PROMISE LAND

MY JOURNEY THROUGH
AMERICA'S
SELF-HELP CULTURE

Jessica Lamb-Shapiro

SIMON & SCHUSTER

New York   London   Toronto   Sydney   New Delhi

Simon & Schuster
1230 Avenue of the Americas
New York, NY 10020

First Simon & Schuster hardcover edition January 2014

SIMON & SCHUSTER and colophon are registered trademarks of Simon & Schuster, Inc.

For information about special discounts for bulk purchases, please contact Simon & Schuster Special Sales at 1-866-506-1949 or business@simonandschuster.com.

The Simon & Schuster Speakers Bureau can bring authors to your live event. For more information or to book an event contact the Simon & Schuster Speakers Bureau at 1-866-248-3049 or visit our website at www.simonspeakers.com.

Interior design: Aline C. Pace
Jacket design: Rex Bonomelli
Jacket photograph © Juniors Bildarchiv GmbH/Alamy

Manufactured in the United States of America

10 9 8 7 6 5 4 3 2 1

Library of Congress Cataloging-in-Publication Data

Lamb-Shapiro, Jessica.
Promise land : my journey through America's self-help culture / Jessica Lamb-Shapiro. — First Simon & Schuster hardcover edition.
    pages   cm
RA776.95.L348 2014
616.890092—dc23   2013011014

ISBN 978-1-4391-0019-6
ISBN 978-1-4391-0160-5 (ebook)

NOTE TO READER

I have mostly used people's real names and descriptions. Where a small degree of anonymity was required, I used people's first names only. Where a greater degree of anonymity was required, I changed first names and one or two small details about their background.

Most of the websites mentioned in this book have changed since I wrote about them, and presumably will continue to change. One or two of them may no longer exist. All quotes and descriptions of websites were accurate at the time that I accessed them.

For my father

The first thing to bear in mind (especially if we ourselves belong to the clerico-academic-scientific type, the officially and conventionally "correct" type, "the deadly respectable" type, for which to ignore others is a besetting temptation) is that nothing can be more stupid than to bar out phenomena from our notice, merely because we are incapable of taking part in anything like them ourselves.

—WILLIAM JAMES, 1902

Most of [self-help] is of a character to repel persons of critical taste. Its language is crude. It makes assertions in regard to scientific matters that cannot be proved. . . . It is mixed up with spiritism, astrology, mind-reading, vegetarianism, reincarnation, and all sorts of other "crank" doctrines and fads—and with a few actual "fakes." The very names of its publications are enough to make sophisticated persons smile.

—FRANCES M. BJÖRKMAN, WRITER/CRITIC, 1910

CONTENTS

PROMISE LAND

ON MISSING THE OBVIOUS

Ten years ago, I tagged along with my father to a weekend conference on how to write self-help books. The conference headliner, Mark Victor Hansen, coauthored *Chicken Soup for the Soul*, one of the most popular and prolific self-help series of the twentieth century, and my father hoped to learn the secrets of his success. A child psychologist by training, my father had been writing self-help books for parents and children for over thirty years, but he had never created a best seller. In college, he studied playwriting, but after penning "several bad plays about the homeless," he switched his major to psychology. Throughout his twenties, he worked as a therapist, but he never gave up on writing. When my mother was pregnant with me, my father began work on his first parenting book, *Games to Grow On*. By the time he was finished I was almost two years old.

On page 100 of *Games*, my father describes "The Perfect Child Game." He instructs the reader to finish the following sentence:

"I want a child who . . ." My father then shares with the reader that when he did this exercise with me in mind, he said, "I want a child who is respectful, listens to me, is happy, is free and creative, is bright, is warm and loving, has good values." He continued, "If I had had more time and had thought about what I was writing, I probably would have put down the same things but reversed their order. I was surprised to see that concern about my little girl's behavior occurred to me before anything else (by the way, she is very well behaved)."*

That was 1979. By the time we went to the conference in 2003, my father had written over forty books and workbooks and started a catalog that sold therapeutic books, games, and toys. Most of his books were self-published and sold through his catalog to schools and psychologists. Four of his books had been published by major houses, but he had never achieved the success of someone like Dr. Phil, a name I picked not at random but because my father particularly despises Dr. Phil (as do, incidentally, many others with Internet access, a facility with Photoshop, and access to a seemingly unlimited cache of devil-themed clip art). I often think of Dr. Phil as my father's bizarro doppelgänger—a middle-aged, mustachioed psychologist who dispenses advice, but who has made a more prosperous living and is devoted to a pop psychology that my father not only disagrees with but feels is ethically irresponsible. My father would probably also point out here that he has more hair than Dr. Phil.

At the conference, my father and I witnessed a pedagogy more befitting a tent revival than a classroom. Mark Victor Hansen proclaimed; his congregants exulted, swooned, and wept. Coming into

---

*It's true; I am very well behaved.

contact with their tumescent, vigorous emotion made me feel alienated, but I also felt pangs of jealousy. I didn't have anything in my life that I felt as passionate about. Even though I had recoiled from self-help and its myriad incarnations my entire life, my interest was piqued. What voodoo made the self-betterment crowd, here and everywhere, so devout? I wanted to know why people liked self-help so much, what it meant to them, whether it worked; and if it didn't work, why people still craved it.

It's nearly impossible to live in the world and escape self-help. We are surrounded all the time by its bastard derivatives. In my local auto body shop, a yellowed sign hanging over the saddest couch in the world proclaims, WE CREATE OUR TOMORROWS BY WHAT WE DREAM TODAY. An e-mail in my in-box tells me to "take heart in this moment and know the best is yet to come." A poster in my hardware store, of a kitten clinging to a tree branch, proffers three simple words: HANG IN THERE.

These axioms may seem like throwaway items, mental tchotchkes that people use to shield themselves from the routine horrors of daily life. They may go unnoticed by us most of the time, but they exist in our peripheral vision, and I am one of those people who believes that we ingest these things accidentally, and that they must have some niggling, if not profound, effect on our psyches, with the most unfathomable consequences. These aphoristic posters and bumper stickers and signs and calendars and pens and e-mails and T-shirts and coffee mugs contain small but constant assurances that the point of view of the universe toward us is not one of overwhelming indifference.

The use of self-help books is a form of bibliotherapy, the idea that a stack of pages between two stiff boards can serve as a therapeutic aid. Self-help books focus on topics affected by our psychology; a book on weight loss is a self-help book, whereas a book on computer programming is not. This can get confusing, however, when they appear together in series like The Complete Idiot's Guide or For Dummies, and because they both use the formal conventions of how-to books.

Self-help is a concept vast and vague enough to include my father's books and board games and sweat lodges and est (a therapy from the 1960s my uncle once tried, where people yelled at you and you weren't allowed to use the bathroom; when I asked him if it had been helpful he said he learned he could hold his urine for a very long time) and *Chicken Soup for the Soul* and Marcus Aurelius and fire walking and Esalen and corporate retreats and tree hugging and addiction support groups and success seminars and self-esteem classes and aspirational calendars that remind you to *be the star of your own life*. Self-help is so simultaneously debunked, adored, and ignored that it's possible to assign any meaning to it you desire. If you hate self-help, it is an exercise in futility that robs fools of their money and dignity. If you love self-help, it is a structure for self-betterment, an opportunity for enlightenment.

As you read this book, try to do something I myself could never quite accomplish: forget what you know, and how you feel, about self-help. Open yourself to the idea that it could be a useful, even necessary, social component; open yourself to the idea that it could also be deceitful and dangerous. Consider what could be beautiful, noble, or enslaving about aspirational living. Consider the possibility that your weird cousin who sends you affirmation-a-day calendars at Christmas may be on to something. Consider the notion that people who think the Omega Institute website is creepy have a point. Just because some self-help books don't fulfill their promises doesn't make the whole genre moronic and doomed. Self-help can be flaky, inarticulate, and illusory, but its longevity, its sheer consistency, suggests it might still have some value in our lives.

Although individual self-help books can be simplistic, self-help itself is complex, contradictory, and hard to pin down. We resist lumping our own unique misery or transcendence with the dumb, hopeless problems of strangers; and at the same time we feel reassured that we are not alone. The concept appeals to our nationalistic notions of self-sufficiency; but the phrase "self-help" carries a stigma among intelligent, educated adults. I think this has something to do with the fact that there will undoubtedly come a time in every intelligent, educated adult's life where they will be helpless and desperate, and this certainty is something we'd all prefer to ignore.

When I began this project, I spent the first few years sitting diligently at the New York Public Library researching self-help books, visiting self-help groups, interviewing self-help purveyors. I amassed pages of notes, which I put into folders, which I put into files. I searched for a Definitive Stance. I began to think of self-help as an entity, an intractable adversary, an almost-being that had some type of relationship to me, a relationship that I was supposed to discern and describe. I wasn't sure how this antagonistic plot was going to end, though it seemed there were limited options: one of us (me or self-help) was going to be revealed as the asshole, and for the sake of a happy ending I was rooting for self-help.

Comprehending this world was less simple and straightforward than I had anticipated. No amount of pressure applied to stacks of self-help books, books about self-help books, or people who self-helped yielded any kind of satisfying clarity. Sometimes it seemed that the more I learned about self-help the more impenetrable it became. There were days when even the phrase sounded strange to me: "self-help," I would mouth, as if, failing to wrap my brain around it, my lips would suffice. I was in a constant state of conflict, overwhelmed by paradox, and in search of a good fainting couch.

Some of the groups and workshops I attended seemed useful and genuine; some didn't. Some of the books I read I admired and enjoyed; some I didn't. There was no truth waiting to be discovered. Eventually, I grew tired of searching, and that's when I realized that I had been stalled at the threshold of something much more personal.

Self-deception is the most intractable deception. I had become preoccupied with whether self-help was good or bad. Why was it so hated or loved? What possible light could old philosophical tracts and etiquette books from ancient Greece or the Victorian era shed on current-day self-actualization? These are problems the mind clings to, to avoid the mind's real trouble. Looking back, it is hard to believe I could spend so much time reading centuries-old self-help books and comparing them to contemporary advice literature, oblivious to the conspicuous direction in which the subject matter was taking me. Yet it took at least four years of wading through copious, unwieldy piles of self-improvement books before I decided to start looking at books on grief, and that was when it began to dawn on me, in the protracted and bovine way that a personal blind spot comes into view, that I was headed toward a very uncomfortable, awkward, and painful conversation with my father.

My mother died just before my second birthday. Instead of memories, I have photos, objects that once belonged to her, and other people's stories. As a child, anytime I looked at a photo or tried on some of her jewelry, I found myself wanting more information. But despite my curiosity, I hated to ask my father about her. I noticed early on that whenever I asked about my mother he became very upset. I took his sadness as a sign that he didn't want to talk; I also found it unbearable. Perhaps once a year the subject would come up naturally, at which point I felt intuitively like I could ask one or two questions. If I ever felt like my father was getting emotional, I changed the subject. Then I would wait another year. Talking about my mother was like looking at the sun; I knew I wasn't supposed to do it, yet I kept sneaking peeks at it every now and then.

In the course of writing this book I walked on hot coals; took a class on how to find a husband; met a man making a weight-loss robot; explained autoerotic asphyxiation to my father; talked to over thirty aspiring self-help writers (one of whom told me I could call him Dr. Huggy Bear, which I very much did not want to do); learned how to write a best-selling self-help book; helped a friend make a vision board; sold mental health products at an Asperger's convention; watched incredibly depressing suicide-prevention videos on the Internet; joined a Healing Circle; ate breakfast with over a hundred grieving children; and faced my debilitating fear of flying.

Of all these things, talking to my father about my mother was by far the hardest. My own ambivalence was the biggest obstacle to opening a door I'd kept shut, locked, and boarded up my whole life. A few years ago, I asked a researcher to find information about my mother, because it seemed easier than talking to someone, anyone, who actually knew her. The researcher's name was also Jessica, which I found auspicious. She unearthed an obituary from a Washington, DC, paper and sent me a pdf. It was the first independent, hard evidence I had of my mother's death. I was oddly elated. Of course it contained only the most generic information. The obit didn't even say how she died, and must have been written by someone in my family, most likely my father. The researcher called the funeral home and was able to confirm my mother's birth and death dates, information I hadn't known—or maybe I had once asked about it and forgotten the answer.

"Your mother was born on March 27th, 1948, and died on July 27th, 1979," the other Jessica wrote me. "Her funeral service was held on Sunday, July 29th. They couldn't give me any further information, as I'm not directly related, but it sounds like they may have more information concerning your mother and possibly more about how she died."

She gave me the phone number; I never called.

1

WE NEED HEART-TOUCHING, SOUL-PENETRATING STORIES!

The Power of Inspirational Tales

March 16, 2003, was a hot and humid day in Atlanta, Georgia, though you wouldn't have known it from within the climate-controlled confines of the Hilton conference room, a location so deep inside the labyrinthine hotel that even the concept of weather seemed remote. My father and I sat in collapsible chairs among six hundred optimistic self-help-book writers, who eagerly awaited the appearance of our hero with a collective glassy-eyed stare that indicated either excitement or fatigue. It was 7 a.m.

The distance between my lungs and fresh air—two ballrooms, a reception area, two escalators, a grand hallway, numerous potted palms, and several rows of automated glass doors—was making me think of death, specifically of how it would feel to be buried alive. My father, on the other hand, waited patiently to learn why Mark Victor Hansen was a multimillionaire and he was not. The thousand-dollar fee (not including the significant cost of hotel rooms and transportation) was one reason. But most attendees professed to not mind spending so much money; as with a real university, they believed the high cost of education was necessary to their success. Unlike at a real university, however, success here was measured by the number of self-help books sold. In this way, the hopeful self-help magnate is a paradoxical breed, at once believing himself to be invested in society's greater good while also desiring to secure a personal shitload of cash.

I went to the conference partly out of curiosity, partly out of habit. I had always tagged along with my father while he worked. At six, I drew the cover of his very first catalog of self-help products, in which I also modeled with a biofeedback machine ($85), wearing a beloved ducky sweater. Flip to page 24, and you will see me pretending to play The Ungame ($15.25), a noncompetitive board game intended to aid "family communication."* Once when my father gave a lecture in England, a friend and I played The Ungame in front of three hundred British mental health professionals to demonstrate how cooperative therapeutic games worked. (We were each paid with a new pair of shoes.) So it seemed normal that I would accompany him to Atlanta for this conference on writing self-help. I was also fresh out of grad school, brokenhearted, and not sure what to do next.

---

*If you are in any way normal, you probably don't know The Ungame, a game that fosters "listening skills as well as self-expression" and "encourages players to describe how they've been affected by frustration, success, excitement, anger, worry, affections, and loneliness." Take a minute to call your parents and thank them for not making you play this game.

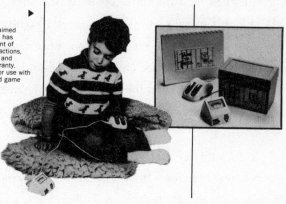

The hotel conference room looked exactly how a hotel conference room should look: chandeliered, windowless, blighted. We sat at long, white-clothed tables facing a black stage flanked by gold balloons; each place setting had a glass of water, a Hilton notebook, a Hilton pen, and a dog bone. We later found out the bone represented our dreams. It didn't take long for me to be struck by the irony of self-help writers being told how to help themselves, as well as the special sadness that attends the relinquishing of authority from an expert to a superexpert. Almost an hour into the introduction, the man we'd come to see was nowhere to be seen, and people were getting restless. Meanwhile, we had learned we must wear our badges at all times, must talk to at least five people at lunch, must not lose our big white binders emblazoned with MVH's grin and purple-shirted torso because *they would not be replaced.*

The attendees varied in age, class, and race, and several had severe physical handicaps. I met a thirteen-year-old boy who was writing a self-help book on surviving adolescence. I stood in an elevator next to a middle-aged man who gripped a headshot of MVH in his metal claw. There were a roughly equal number of men and women. Like the lottery, the business of writing self-help is equal opportunity; the chance that one might win, however remote, is enough to keep the system functioning. Everyone here believed they had a chance at success and, at least technically, they were correct.

As we waited for MVH to appear, most everyone, my father included, took copious notes on minor logistical topics like the hours of operation for tiki bar chain Trader Vic's. I peeked over at my father's notepad; it said, "drinking opportunities."

Suddenly the lights dimmed and the crowd quieted. Speakers blasted Tina Turner's "Simply the Best." The emcee said, dramatically:

Introducing the man,
The living legend,
The person who made the word "mega" mean something . . .*

Mark Victor Hansen bounded onto the stage. The audience erupted in wild enthusiasm, jumping out of their chairs; there were shouts of "yeah!" and "yea-uhh!" MVH crossed the stage more like an NBA star than a middle-aged, balding self-help guru, pump-

---

*Some thoughts on the word "mega," used at the conference with zealous dedication. First, mega is not so much a word as a prefix, taken from a Greek word that means "large." MVH slapped this prefix indiscriminately, one might say promiscuously, on every noun in sight. The conference was called the MEGA Book Marketing University; MVH spoke not of success, but of megasuccess. Contrary to the claim that he made the word mega "mean something," I would argue MVH's overuse of the word made it mean very little.

ing his arms up and down in a gesture I am pretty sure the kids call "raising the roof." Standing tall at 6' 4", the man who called himself "The Authority on Human Potential" had a penchant for purple dress shirts. He was wearing one now, as in most photos. He later revealed that purple is the highest color on the electromagnetic spectrum. There is a reason behind every decision MVH makes, and most of it is heavily based on market research (FYI: the number seven is also "very powerful").

"Information is the most profitable product in the world," intoned MVH, with funereal seriousness. He then told us the story of Chicken Soup. The first book, *Chicken Soup for the Soul*, was a collection of feel-good stories about individual success and triumph over adversity. Since then, the Chicken Soup book buyer has been offered Chicken Soup stories for every conceivable collective: moms, scuba divers, stamp collectors, abuse survivors, Christians, hockey fans, dog people, cat people, breast cancer survivors, married people, back pain sufferers, stressed people, brides, teens, preteens, Canadians, country music fans, grandmothers, runners, teachers, college students, golfers, twins, divorcées, empty nesters, Black people, Jewish people, Latinos, caregivers, dieters, entrepreneurs, gardeners, menopausal women, dentists, ocean lovers, and veterans.

The story of how he and partner Jack Canfield came to publish their first book was the first of innumerable inspirational tales we would hear that weekend, and it seemed fitting that their narrative of publishing inspirational stories was itself an inspirational story. The bread and butter of the Chicken Soup empire, and almost all self-help narratives, is the inspirational story. In fact, over the course of the weekend I would hear this particular story from various people more than twenty times, and each time the number of New York publishers who rejected the book got higher (highest: 144), and the number of copies sold got larger (largest: seventeen million), and the payoff got concomitantly better.

I will admit to you right now that I quickly grew to love this story, and, furthermore, that it ignited in me an exponentially growing urge to shout, IN YOUR FACE! As such, I submit to you that these predictable and formally drab success narratives, while bizarre and improbable, are unhateable. A man returns home to find his wife and children dead; feeling his life has no purpose, about to commit suicide, he rescues a baby from a swimming pool and reaffirms his usefulness in the world. A nurse works in a hospital caring for "cripples" when a crane smashes through the window and paralyzes her; now she lobbies against the government and is famous and rich. Yes, the ways in which these stories manipulate our emotional response are evident, yet, despite such knowledge, the formula works. These stories are tiny units of powerful emotional incitement. Even for a cynical reader, is there not something potentially chord-touching in these stories? Do you hate babies and cripples?

MVH employed the same technique used in his books to emotionally ignite and detonate his audience. With Pollyannaish optimism, he shared story after story of turning tragedy into triumph, lemons into lemonade. For instance, did you know that Sylvester Stallone wrote *Rocky* in three days? That it was turned down by "every major Hollywood producer"? That some bonehead wanted to cast Robert Redford as Rocky? (This gem elicited many a horrified gasp.) Did you know that Stallone sold it for nothing on the condition that he would play the lead? Did you know that David fought Goliath with only one stone? MVH used this exact story sequence to incite zealous, if slightly unfocused, fervor in his audience: he paced the stage, he waved his hands emphatically, the purple shirt shagged back and forth, he insisted we sing the *Rocky* theme song. Truly terrible humming and DA-da-da-DA-da-DA-da-da-DA-ing ensued. Some people were confused and sang "Eye of the Tiger."

MVH's never-say-die ethos was dubious but seductive. After all, there is a theory behind the power of the inspirational story, implicit (and often outright acknowledged) in almost every self-help book since pre-Biblical times: that hearing about other people's success gives us hope, and hope is the backbone of perseverance and triumph. Have you ever noticed that when you encounter misfortune many people will tell you a similar story from their own lives? That 99 percent of the time the moral of said similar story is that they overcame said similar situation and, most probably, you will too? MVH encouraged us to "start from where you're vulnerable; it endears you to the audience." The power of these stories, according to MVH, could not be overestimated; he insisted, "We *need* heart-touching, soul-penetrating stories!"

The inspirational story appears in all self-help topics, from personal finance to weight loss to overcoming addiction to spiritual renewal to marriage to child rearing. The message of the inspirational story has nothing to do with subject or specifics; it simply says, "If that guy can do it, why can't you?" Our country's founding document tells us that all men are created equal, which we often mistake for meaning that we all have the same abilities. We indisputably don't; yet inspirational stories repeatedly tell us that if one person can accomplish something, anyone can. To contradict this would be to contradict one of the founding tenets of the American Dream. In 1840, Alexis de Tocqueville noted the logical flaw in America's promise of equal opportunity when he wrote,

> The same equality that allows every citizen to conceive these lofty hopes renders all the citizens less able to realize them; it circumscribes their powers on every side, while it gives freer scope to their desires.

In 1882, William Mather, a British professor, lawyer, and journalist, wrote of "success" books, "From the general spirit of these appeals, one would suppose the writers to believe that every human being at birth is potentially a Shakespeare or a Newton, and that, provided he is educated properly, and labors long and hard enough, he may astonish the world with 'Hamlets' and 'Principias.'"

The inspirational story is so ubiquitous it has subgenres: rags-to-riches tales, Horatio Alger Jr. stories, Cinderella stories, ugly duckling stories. Your classic I.S. looks like this:

> Human in desperate, objectively bad situation—Makes accidental yet somehow fated discovery—Has epiphany—Pursues line of activity based on epiphany—Becomes wildly successful—Overcomes desperate, objectively bad situation.

Many of today's most popular self-help books begin with the author at an incredibly low point. Consider the second sentence of contemporary best seller *The Power of Now*: "Until my thirtieth year, I lived in a state of almost continuous anxiety interspersed with periods of suicidal depression."

Our hunger for inspirational stories is nothing new. Ancient Egypt had a genre called "Sebayt," an instructional literature on life (Sebayt means "teachings"). Stoic philosophers Seneca, Marcus Aurelius, and Epictetus frequently mixed anecdotes with maxims on how to live, and works by these three authors can still be found in the self-help section of your local bookstore.* Sections of the Bible like the book of Job, Proverbs, and Ecclesiastes use parables to guide the reader's behavior (Tyndale House Publishers even offers a Bible "self-help edition"). During the Early Middle Ages, Middle Ages, and Renaissance, mirror-of-princes books told stories of kings whose behavior should be imitated or avoided. Conduct books, which told men how to behave in polite society, were popular in Italy, France, and England during the seventeenth and eighteenth centuries. Horatio Alger Jr.'s popular fictions in the late nineteenth century featured stories of upward mobility and per-

---

*Aurelius's inspirational offerings carry a bleak undertone. He believed life was so fleeting we shouldn't waste our energy on what later became known as "the small stuff." He achieves this message by expressing ceaselessly that you and everyone you know are, seriously and without a doubt, going to die. Here is but a small sample: "Remind yourself constantly of all the physicians, now dead"; "Hippocrates cured the ills of many, but he himself took ill and died"; "Of all that life, not a trace survives today"; " 'A poor soul burdened with a corpse,' Epictetus calls you"; "Yesterday a drop of semen, tomorrow a handful of spice or ashes"; "Think of Destiny, and how puny a part of it you are"; "That men of a certain type should behave as they do is inevitable. To wish it otherwise were to wish that the fig-tree would not yield its juice. In any case, remember that in a very little while both you and he will be dead and your very names will quickly be forgotten"; "Very soon you will be dead."

sonal triumph, where merit was prized over inherited privilege, and a person of modest or no means could succeed through ingenuity, education, talent. Titles like *Jed, the Poorhouse Boy* and *Ragged Dick* cued the reader toward his characters' low beginnings.

In 1863, an inspirational story of losing weight, William Banting's *Letter on Corpulence,* became an instant hit. Banting, a portly man with a kind face, was a "fashionable London undertaker," and was known for having made the Duke of Wellington's coffin. At age sixty-five Banting weighed 202 lb., could not tie his own shoes, and had to climb down stairs backward. By following a protein-and-liquor-centric diet of his own design he lost nearly fifty pounds.* He addressed *Letter on Corpulence* to the public, saying his only motive was a sincere wish to help his "fellow creatures." He so strongly believed in his mission that he gave away the first 2,500 copies.

More than individuals of any prior era, Victorians embraced the tenets of progress, discipline, and self-betterment. During the Industrial Revolution, people moved to cities in record numbers. As modern living became chaotic and baffling, Victorians searched for structure and order. Self-help provided this, as well as a way to organize and disseminate knowledge. During the 1850s there was a surge in success literature on both sides of the Atlantic, designed to provide readers with useful knowledge about navigating urban and industrial life and to suggest tactics for "getting on";

---

*He recommends five ounces of meat, fish, or kidneys for breakfast, with tea and a little biscuit; for lunch, five or six ounces of any fish (except salmon or herring), meat (except pork or veal), "fruit out of a pudding," and two or three glasses of claret or sherry (beer and champagne are "forbidden"); for dinner, three or four ounces of meat or fish, similar to lunch, and a nightcap (one or two glasses of sherry).

the mid-nineteenth century saw many books like Samuel Smiles's *Self-Help* (1859), encouraging readers to follow a prescripted path to self-improvement.*

Samuel Smiles grew up in Scotland, the eldest of eleven children. A writer for the *Leeds Times*, he was approached by the Mutual Improvement Society in 1845 to give a talk, later published under the title "The Education of the Working Classes." *Self-Help*, a prototypical *Chicken Soup for the Soul*, was a collection of inspirational stories about working-class men rising to power. Mixing precept and anecdote, *Self-Help* chronicled the lives of men who succeeded against all odds. Smiles felt these examples of what other men had done were "illustrations of what each might, in a greater or less degree, do for himself."

Smiles believed in the stories' ability to promote change; he writes that, after attending his lecture, "the youths went forward in their course; worked on with energy and resolution; and, reaching manhood, they went forth in various directions into the world, where many of them now occupy positions of trust and usefulness." Smiles wrote in his autobiography that the purpose of his stories was to "illustrate and enforce the power of [. . .] PERSEVERANCE." If "enforce" seems like a bizarre word choice here, it most likely reflects the Victorian fanaticism for uplifting society, but it could also argue for the didactic potential of parables. Biographies, rather than simply stories of individual lives, were regarded as demonstrations of "what men can be, and what they can do." Indeed, each story repeats the narrative structure of a man who "sprang from the ranks" and ends up the "founder of the modern factory

---

Self-Help is often cited as the first self-help book, and is the first book to use the words in its title.

system" or sets an example for "the whole cotton trade" or makes an "astonishing achievement, which may be pronounced almost unequaled in the history of mechanical invention!"

Like *Chicken Soup for the Soul*, *Self-Help* was initially rejected (by Routledge in 1855). Smiles self-published using his own money in 1859, and the book became a sweeping best seller, moving 20,000 units. By 1900 it had sold more than a quarter of a million copies. *Self-Help* was published in the same year as *The Origin of Species*; Smiles outsold Darwin. The only book *Self-Help* didn't outsell that year was the Bible.

Certainly the ever-growing Chicken Soup audience attests to the perennial power of inspirational stories: The series, which began in 1995, has by now sold over 112 million copies, has been translated into over forty languages, and has almost two hundred titles in print. Mark Victor Hansen and cocreator Jack Canfield hold the Guinness World Record for having the most books on the *New York Times* best-seller list at one time (seven books, May 1998). They even created a Chicken Soup branded dog and cat food (if you ever want to see photos of white people hugging dogs, this is your website). MVH was completely unapologetic about his financial success; to him, it only indicated how much need there was for his product. "In case you ain't got it," said MVH, "I'm pro-capitalism and free enterprise. My immigrant parents came from Denmark—" Here MVH was cut off by wild applause, either for capitalism or free enterprise or Denmark.

Along with the inspirational story, MVH employed the second favorite rhetorical arm-twist of self-help: the imperative. "Who's going to build the information empire? Point to your neighbor and say 'I see you doing it!'" I looked at the gray-suited man on my left. I pointed weakly to Gray Suit even though, given that he was teary-eyed and breathing funny, I didn't really see him doing it.

Lorrie Moore's story collection *Self-Help*, in which she frequently uses the imperative tense, demonstrates why oversimplified instructions are not necessarily the best tool for confronting human suffering. In "The Kid's Guide to Divorce," she writes,

> Try groaning root beer, root beer, like a dying cowboy you saw on a commercial once, but drink the water anyway. When you are no longer choking, your face is less red, and you can breathe again, ask for a Coke. Your mom will say: I don't think so; Dr. Atwood said your teeth were atrocious.
>
> Tell her Dr. Atwood is for the birds.

The imperative highlights the avoidance of the titular divorce; it isn't mentioned until the last paragraph, and then only briefly: "Leave out the part about the lady and the part about the beer." Moore at once directs our attention to how safe and comforting the imperative is as a mode—not to mention a relief from personal accountability—while pointing to its obfuscating potential.

MVH was an enthusiast of the imperative, which he abused frequently in order to make adults, myself included, do a number of surprising things. By the end of those first two hours on Saturday morning he had whipped the audience into a religious fervor:

MVH: Say, "I'm ready."
AUDIENCE: I'm ready!

MVH: Say, "I recognize my gift!"

A: I recognize my gift!

MVH: Say, "I love selling it!"

A: I love selling it!

MVH: Here's another great reason to be an author. It's an impressive career. Say, "I'm an author."

A: I'm an author!*

MVH: J. K. Rowling is richer than the queen of England! Say, "That's me!"

A: That's me!

MVH: Touch yourself and say, "I've got permission."

A: [interpreting "touch yourself" in various discomfiting ways] I've got permission!

His call-and-response was punctuated by occasional shouts of "Amen" and Hansen's admission that he "prayed to the Lord last night that [we] would be successful." At this point, if he'd commanded us to say, "I'm a rhinoceros," and gore our Hilton notepads with imaginary horns, we most likely would have complied. It may come as no surprise, then, that toward the end of the lecture, when MVH commanded us to grab another person's index finger and draw a smiley face on the tip, we did. I gingerly pinched Gray Suit's finger; he grabbed mine with gusto. If you have never drawn a smiley face on a stranger's finger, suffice it to say that it is uncomfortably intimate.

"Say, 'I see that's you,'" MVH directed.

---

*Side note: part of the MEGA Book Marketing University's rhetorically dynamic lexicon is the use of "author" instead of "writer." The reason for this is that an author does not necessarily write books; MVH is the *author* of the Chicken Soup series but does not *write* them.

"I see that's you," we droned.

Several people around me were now openly crying, men and women alike. As I watched them, tears streaking their faces, they rubbed their heads and said in unison, "This is wisdom." I glanced at my watch; it wasn't even noon.

The scene was perplexing, but also unexpectedly moving. These people were here because they desperately wanted something, and, by the looks of it, Mark Victor Hansen was giving it to them. It didn't take long to figure out that the inspirational story was a psychological machine of fantasy that turns tragedy into triumph, and makes meaning out of the meaningless. MVH was selling a vision of happiness and hope that grinned unabashedly in the face of disappointment and decay. I considered another reason why we were all vulnerable to the pleasures of the imperative. I had been told what to do, wear, and eat for the last two hours, and it brought me a kind of comfort. It was no accident, I thought, that the last time I had this little responsibility for my actions I had braces on my teeth, a bona fide mullet, and someone to cook me dinner every night.

After our introduction to the conference, we spilled out into a large hallway lined with tables advertising editing help, website design, and other amenities a future self-help empire might need to thrive. I chatted up some fellow attendees. Although a few felt dissatisfied by the first two hours of sybaritic splendor accompanied by scant concrete instruction, the majority of them were pleased. The word "energy" was bandied about gratuitously. This "energy," by which I guessed people meant hope or a sense of personal promise, seemed to be exactly what they had been searching for. Melissa had no book or even a title yet, but she said, "The conference is profound. The synergy, the energy in the room, it's so exciting. Profound; that's the only word for it." (I would say about a third of the people I interviewed were like Melissa: young, enthusiastic, directionless.) Behind me, a man on his cell phone shouted, "I'm so excited, I had to call you!"

Hansen's stories had fueled the crowd's ebullience like a bellows stokes a fire. The word "inspire" refers to breath—literally "to breathe into," as when you resuscitate a dying person by breathing into their mouth, and metaphorically *to give life.* This is the great paradox of self-help; at the same time as people are feeling inspired, as new life is breathed into them, they are also becoming dependent on the person or book or program that is providing the air. Once you are hooked up to the oxygen machine, you have to drag it with you wherever you go.

Connie, a mother of five from Celebration, Florida, sporting a turquoise pantsuit and a large Jesus-themed ring, said the conference was "very helpful." I asked her how she liked living in Celebration, a town invented by Disney, modeled after a vision of Main Street, U.S.A. Connie told me that she loved it, that she found it ideal.

> ME: What's your book about?
> C: Making homemaking fun, using Disney principles.
> For example, have an "opening time." Disney World has an opening time, and there's that magic of walking into the empty park, all set up and ready for fun.
> ME: What's your opening time?
> C: Nine a.m.
> ME: You must get up awfully early.
> C: Yes.
> ME: And what's involved in getting ready for the "opening"?

C: Lots of vacuuming. Mostly cleaning. Straightening
     pillows on the couch. [pause] Sometimes I get tired.

ME: I'm tired just talking about it.

C: But then in the morning the world is clean; magical
     dreams come true.

ME: I guess so.

C: [sighing and looking heavenward] I love Disney.

On Saturday afternoon MVH's agent, Jillian Manus, told us about another unlikely brainchild—this one already proven successful. "Knitting with dog hair," she shrieked. "I thought it was the worst idea in the world. But you know what? This lady thought of all the people with dogs and all the people who knit . . ." She trailed off while the audience put two and two together, wolf-smiling as they collectively gasped with delight, probably thinking: Shit, I could do better than *that*.

Dale Carnegie's *How to Win Friends and Influence People* is one of the best-known self-help books to the 20th-century reader. (Carnegie's other, lesser-known books are *How to Stop Worrying and Start Living* and *Lincoln the Unknown*.) Carnegie changed the spelling of his name from the original Carnagey, perhaps to suggest he might be related to the steel magnate Andrew Carnegie. In reality, Dale Carnegie was born on a Missouri farm into a poor family. At college he could not afford room and board and had to ride horseback from home to his classes daily. First drawn to sales, he then made a brief attempt at a career in acting. In 1912, he found himself jobless in New York City, where he talked the local YMCA into letting him lecture on public speaking. Carnegie did minimal speaking himself, asking the students to perform impromptu lectures instead. Soon he was publishing how-to books on public speaking. He approached Simon & Schuster many times about publishing his techniques, and they finally acquiesced in 1936.

In only a few months, Simon & Schuster published fourteen editions of *How to Win Friends and Influence People.* It was the number-one best seller in 1937, with 729,000 copies sold. By 1956, the book had sold five million copies in hardcover and paperback. It's still in print today.

Carnegie's best seller has confident chapter titles like "The Big Secret of Dealing with People," "How to Make People Like You Instantly," and "If You Don't Do This, You're Headed for Trouble." Carnegie micromanages your success down to the reading of his own book, with "Nine Suggestions on How to Get the Most Out of This Book." But before all that, Carnegie begins with an inspirational story, unrepentantly working the oldest narrative ploy for sympathy:

Did you ever stop to think that a dog is the only animal that doesn't have to work for a living? A hen has to lay eggs, a cow has to give milk, and a canary has to sing. But a dog makes his living by giving you nothing but love.

When I was five years old, my father bought a little yellow-haired pup for fifty cents. He was the light and joy of my childhood. Every afternoon about four-thirty, he would sit in the front yard with his beautiful eyes staring steadfastly at the path, and as soon as he heard my voice or saw me swinging my dinner pail through the buck brush, he was off like a shot, racing breathlessly up the hill to greet me with leaps of joy and barks of sheer ecstasy.

Tippy was my constant companion for five years. Then one tragic night—I shall never forget it—he was killed within ten feet of my head, killed by lightning. Tippy's death was the tragedy of my boyhood.

You never read a book on psychology, Tippy. You didn't need to. You knew by some divine instinct that you can make more friends in two months by becoming genuinely interested in other people than you can in two years by trying to get other people interested in you. Let me repeat that. You can make more friends in two months by becoming interested in other people than you can in two years by trying to get other people interested in you.

There are myriad reasons why this may be the most genius narrative sell ever, and I will list only a few: the box-office-gold "a dog makes his living by giving you nothing but love"; the protagonist is a five-year-old child; "pup" in place of "puppy"; the phrases "dinner pail," "buck brush," "leaps of joy," and "barks of sheer ecstasy" all in one sentence; the dog's name is Tippy; the repetition of "killed" in "killed within ten feet of my head, killed by lightning"; the heart-rending shift to second person and present tense in the last paragraph, where a grown man talks to his lost dog somewhere *beyond the grave*; and the fact that Carnegie seamlessly moves from doggie death to the point of his book in two sentences, a transition that you have to admire for its sentence-length-to-emotional-distance-traveled ratio.

Published at the tail end of the Great Depression, this type of book was especially attractive to people, historians argue, because it encouraged them to believe success could be achieved through the one thing they had not lost: themselves. This in fact may be what attracts writers to self-help—expertise is based on personal experience, and as such you can pretty much write a self-help book about anything.

On Saturday, at MVH's first "networking lunch," my father and I sat with Reecy, a college finance maven; Brenda Star, an iridologist (someone who diagnoses physical and emotional illness by looking at your irises); Cristy, who practiced something called "ontological design"; a woman who rolled her eyes at everything; and Dr. Darcy, a sex therapist. Dr. Darcy broke the ice with a lively discussion of herpes and chlamydia.

"One-third of all people have an STD," she announced omnidirectionally, "And 25 percent of all teens!"

Everyone scrutinized their pasta primavera, including my father and I, who were perhaps more than anyone super desperate to avoid eye contact.

"That's a lot," said the eye-roller.

My dad and Reecy, the only men at the table, looked annoyed. Brenda Star smiled politely, stared into middle space, and fingered the wooden animal menagerie strung around her neck.

"Everyone here gets a free sex question," Dr. Darcy announced cheerily. Dr. Darcy looked about thirty, with short brown hair and a baby face. Unlike many of the attendees, she had already written and self-published a book, *Virgin S-E-X,* about how to make your deflowering a "positive experience." Reecy changed the subject by giving Dr. Darcy tips on college financing for her kids but refused the sex advice proffered in return. We were all profoundly grateful to him.

Our lunch crew also hypothesized about formulas for success, particularly book titles and covers. Mahesh Grossman, another conference lecturer, told us later that day that there were two titles guaranteed not to fail: What __ Knows About __ That __ Should

Know, and anything with a number in it (25 Ways to __). To wit: one of the tables outside the lecture hall displayed *25 Ways to Feeling Good*, and a book called *What Southern Women Know (That All Women Should)*. Chapter titles like "Always Look Your Best Even If You Feel Your Worst" suggest possible explanations why this particular Yankee remains unwed.

———

The reliance on formulas, both for writing self-help books and for the transformations of their readers, is crucial to the inspirational story. Formulas explain to the reader how individual success can translate into a universally replicable salvation. An exemplar of the link between formulas and self-betterment comes in Benjamin Franklin's *Autobiography*, which both Dale Carnegie and Tony Robbins have cited as an inspiration, and which Davy Crockett kept by his bedside during the final siege of the Alamo. Franklin states in his introduction:

> Having emerg'd from the Poverty & Obscurity in which I was born & bred, to a State of Affluence & some Degree of Reputation in the World, and having gone so far thro' Life with a considerable Share of Felicity, the conducing Means I made use of, which, with the Blessing of God, so well succeeded, my Posterity may like to know, as they may find some of them suitable to their own Situations, & *therefore fit to be imitated*. [my emphasis]

Franklin could be the poster child for the American myth of self-creation. He was a boy who, without inherited wealth, formal education, or family connections, rose to a position of wealth and influence, using only his hard work, pluck, and ingenuity. It is no accident that his face, of all possible historical figures, graces America's highest note of currency. *Autobiography* reads like a market report on success: an approach, replete with lists, charts, and graphs, that reflects Franklin's proclivity for scientific method. Upon isolating which, exactly, the indispensible virtues are (there are thirteen), Franklin lists them in greater detail, elaborating, for instance, on what he means by SILENCE:

> Speak not but what may benefit others or yourself. Avoid trifling Conversation.

Also, INDUSTRY:

> Lose no Time. Be always employ'd in something useful. Cut off all unnecessary Actions.

CLEANLINESS:

> Tolerate no Uncleanness in Body, Clothes, or Habitation.

CHASTITY:

> Rarely use Venery but for Health or Offspring; Never to Dullness, Weakness, or the Injury of your own or another's Peace or Reputation.

Concluding finally with HUMILITY, which according to Franklin means:

> Imitate Jesus and Socrates.

Franklin also offers a chart whereby he and his reader can daily, weekly, and monthly record displays of Virtues. So that you will not be overwhelmed, Franklin simply suggests that you track one Virtue a week, and that after thirteen weeks of recording your displays of Virtue, you begin again, and so on and so forth, indefinitely.

TEMPERANCE. *Eat not to Dulness Drink not to Elevation.*							
	S	M	T	W	T	F	S
T							
S	●●	●		●		●	
O	●	●	●		●	●	●
R			●			●	
F		●			●		
I		●					
S							
J							
M							
Cl.							
T							
Ch.							
H							

On Sunday, the second and final day of the conference, Mark Victor Hansen divulged a less scientific formula for our writing: REAL WEALTH = IDEAS + ENERGY. He paused a few moments to let the gravitas of this formula seep in. Projected onto a monolithic white screen, an intractable problem made solvable math equation, it seemed so easy. "Stay focused," he told us, followed by the sound of six hundred people furiously scribbling, *Stay focused.* "I learned that lesson from Colin Powell. Focus. That's how we won the war in 1992." My dad and I exchanged a familial eyebrow raise; then he pretended to strangle himself, while I shot at him with an invisible machine gun.

MVH offered his own success like the proverbial carrot for our gimpy, malnourished horse. Even his website favored words like "riches" and "empire," and featured inspirational stories from the gold-rush age, stories that recalled an "olde" and largely uncomplicated American ideology of success-for-all. MVH's website proclaimed him "America's Ambassador of Possibility":

> In the area of human potential, no one is better known or more respected than Mark Victor Hansen. . . . When Mark is not speaking, writing or marketing his next bestselling book, he and his wife Patty live in Newport Beach, California with their daughters Elisabeth and Melanie. Together, the family nurtures dozens of chickens, 8 pigeons, 5 cats, 5 dogs, 3 rabbits, a multitude of fish, 4 horses, 1 peacock, 1 hamster and an organic garden complete with fruit, vegetables, herbs and is full of hummingbirds, butterflies and wonderfully fragrant flowers. Mark Victor Hansen is an enthusiastic crusader of what's possible and is driven to make the world a better place.

MVH doesn't have flowers; he has "wonderfully fragrant flowers." For any of us still too dim to comprehend his level of achievement, his website had a photo gallery, where anyone interested could see him doing things that only the cash-laden do: sailing and hugging celebrities. I scrolled through pictures of MVH with notables like Wayne Gretzky; Leeza Gibbons; that guy who dates Oprah; Clarence Thomas; and the artist LeRoy Neiman, taken in a Las Vegas hotel, where LeRoy Neiman sports a Dali-type mustache three times the diameter of his head and wears a white bathrobe (did MVH surprise him in the pool? the shower?). MVH's familiar smile is near-decayed, his eyes mimicking the half surprise of a felon in a police raid, a look that suggests MVH is not so happy about posing for a picture with a bathrobed, mustachioed man as he might like you to think.

MVH insisted that his books—and the larger enterprise that surrounded them—were vehicles to "bring good" to the people of the world. During the conference, he urged us to donate our toiletries to homeless shelters, to give blood, said, "When Solomon talked to God, he asked for *influence*, to feed the hungry. My mission is to feed the hungry." MVH was rebuilding a corroded wailing wall; MVH wanted to "elevate the IP (Information Product) of the world"; MVH's personal motto was "I'm here to serve." He told us that we needed to write for the LDCs (Less Developed Countries), that they "depend on us."

Throughout the entire weekend every time a guest speaker entered or left the stage Sister Sledge's "We Are Family" played, and hugging so serious and intimate ensued that it made me feel like a peeping Tom. MVH also wanted us to know how inspirational he was in his everyday life; he shared personal gems like "I took my Pueblo housekeeper to the gynecologist; she said, 'He wants to look at WHAT?'" This unexpected little joke seemed significant given the proliferation of birthing metaphors MVH used for the writing process: we were "like ob-gyns"; we should "keep track of our babies"; and at one point he showed us a slide of Michelangelo's David holding a Chicken Soup book over his genitals—symbolism as layered and disturbing as any I ever encountered in a college literature class.

Central to the potential goodness of these publications is the notion that books have transformative therapeutic powers with concrete, real-world results. MVH insisted they could: "We wrote

Chicken Soup for the Prisoner's Soul. . . . These people used to want to kill; not anymore!" *Chicken Soup for the Soul Bible*? "It's going to get more people to read the Bible!" MVH seemed sincere in the belief that his books mattered to any and every social group: "Teenagers, they said, Mark, we want a book on abuse, 'cause we're abused! So I gave it to them. And it sold millions of copies in the first few weeks." Janet Switzer, another lecturer, echoed this sentiment in a less generous way: "You're not selling books; you're selling a vision for what their life could be like once they buy your information, your program, your system."

———

One consistent criticism of self-help is that it is too pat, too regulatory, too mechanical. Franklin's list of virtues, for instance, does not attempt to plumb the depths of human experience, preferring to skim the pragmatic surface of daily living. He repeatedly eschews the philosophical for the practical. D. H. Lawrence once railed against Franklin, "I'm not going to be turned into a virtuous little automaton as Benjamin would have me. . . . He tries to take away my wholeness, my dark forest, my freedom." In suggesting that one formula works for all people, Franklin denies individuals their diversity, their idiosyncrasy, their uniqueness—in essence, what makes the self a self. To accept this would be to trade in one's blessed peculiarity for a mere "vision" of "what your life could be like."

But the most tragic shortcoming of the inspirational true story is that, like the people they depict, the stories are rooted in a specific time and place, and shifts in context can irrevocably damage or obscure their meaning. Interpretation becomes problematic, even in a true story; since the meaning of a story is neither self-evident nor fixed, the moral and subsequent course of action can't be either. This congenital defect is well-illustrated by the following inspirational story, published in the very first *Chicken Soup for the Soul*, Dan Clark's "Make It Come True."

In 1957 a ten-year-old boy in California set a goal. At the time Jim Brown was the greatest running back ever to play pro football and this tall, skinny boy wanted his autograph. In order to accomplish his goal, the young boy had to overcome some obstacles.

He grew up in the ghetto, where he never got enough to eat. Malnutrition took its toll, and a disease called rickets forced him to wear steel splints to support his skinny, bowed-out legs. He had no money to buy a ticket to get into the game, so he waited patiently near the locker room until the game ended and Jim Brown left the field. He politely asked Brown for his autograph. As Brown signed, the boy explained, "Mr. Brown, I have your picture on my wall. I know you hold all the records. You're my idol."

Brown smiled and began to leave, but the young boy wasn't finished. He proclaimed, "Mr. Brown, one day I'm going to break every record you hold!" Brown was impressed and asked, "What is your name, son?"

The boy replied, "Orenthal James. My friends call me O. J."

O. J. Simpson went on to break all but three of the rushing records held by Jim Brown before injuries shortened his football career. Goal setting is the strongest force for human motivation. Set a goal and make it come true.

This inspirational story was published in 1993; in 1994, Simpson's ex-wife, Nicole, and her friend Ronald Goldman were murdered.

Mark Victor Hansen's MEGA Book Marketing University was a gathering of earnest, likable people; yet there was something inherently suspicious and increasingly menacing about the unrelenting claims that we were all going to be winners and help people. I heard almost every speaker, at least once in their talk, lower their voice and say, without irony, "But can I be honest with you?" And although we were all supposed to be equally successful, we competed for information (read: bought more products); when MVH offered spots in a "protégé" program after his Sunday lecture, audience members nearly trampled each other to rush to the first fifty seats.

We were told: "Don't be a tire kicker. If you're a tire kicker, you're not going to get anything out of this." This was very different from an actual university, where most students are encouraged to turn their critical faculties on both themselves and what they are taught. Further, in an actual university one eventually graduates; whereas here it seemed that the potential for attending seminars and buying inspirational tapes was endless. My father and I estimated that by the end of the weekend MVH had made more than $200,000. MVH himself at one point bragged, "When I sleep, I know I'm making money in China." Indeed, MVH's success is based on the proliferation of one product. Series like Chicken Soup have huge profit potential because the audience is preselected and the writers (distinct from authors) are often poorly paid, if paid at all.

As part of his closing remarks on Sunday, MVH told us the best lesson he learned was from George Lucas:

> MVH: Everyone say, "series."
> EVERYONE: Series.

MVH: Everyone say, "sequel."

E: Sequel.

MVH: Everyone say, "prequel!"

E: Prequel!

MVH: It's all about the series: [screaming] chicken, chicken, chicken!

Yet Marilyn, an attractive older woman with a first-rate blond dye job, insisted the Chicken Soup model worked for her. She seemed bright and funny, and had been to four of these conferences. Marilyn told me that these programs "underpromise and overdeliver. They make you think outrageous. You feel empowered, like you can make a difference. Education is empowerment." And all of the money changing hands for this education and empowerment? "I believe that the best way to help the poor is not to be one of them."

My father's most successful book was published by Harper-Collins, and it was the highlight of his career in self-help. "They sent me a credit card with my name on it. That was so cool. They treated me like someone special—which is a rare occurrence in this life. But then I would go to bookstores and have the opposite experience. I went to a small bookstore in Los Angeles to do a book signing, and there was no one there. *No one.* There was a rep from Harper with me, and I asked her, 'What should I do?' She said, 'Can you just go around and talk to people?' I said, 'About what?' But I did it. Another time, I was at a Barnes & Noble, and there was also a reading by Cal Ripken Jr. There were stacks of his book, piles everywhere, and they were five feet high! And all these signs, saying, 'Don't Touch Cal,' 'Don't Look at Cal.' I kept looking for the sign that said, 'We Don't Care What You Do to Dr. Shapiro; We're Just Glad You Showed Up.' So on the one hand I felt like a big shot, and on the other I was having these demoralizing experiences."

While the conference may have aided Marilyn and countless others, it disillusioned my father. It failed to solve the puzzle of how to write a best-selling self-help book. It failed to motivate him to keep trying. The sheer multitude of fellow strivers only convinced him how unlikely his chances of making it were. Worse, hearing someone else's blind confidence in their profoundly ludicrous scheme only heightens the nagging suspicion that one's own ideas might be equally risible.

For my father, this conference had been a last hope. He had been promised that there was a code to MVH's success, which, once cracked, would grant him equal access to the self-help market, and equal prosperity. That promise turned out to be a lie. There was no secret to learn, only more of MVH's products to buy. No success, only more striving toward an ever-receding horizon point. MVH's example did not feel inspirational; it was dispiriting and depressing. So, in what seemed like a symbolic gesture, my father enacted the greatest possible rebuke in a capitalist society: he asked for his money back.

To MVH's credit, he stood by his "complete satisfaction" money-back guarantee. Three months later, my father received a full refund. He also got back the eight hundred dollars he had paid for my ticket, but there must have been some computer error because I began to receive peculiar trinkets in the mail, like a silver-plated platter inscribed with WHO SAYS NOTHING IS EVER HANDED TO YOU ON A SILVER PLATTER? Ten years later, I still get e-mails from MVH. I am told emphatically that "*Literary agents* are looking for your book. Don't participate in the recession. This event will change your life!" Very few topics are not within his purview. "Jessica, are you a healthepreneur?" reads one subject line. Mark Victor Hansen wants to know, "Jessica, are you single?" The frequency of e-mails grew in proportion to the decline of the economy; by 2009 I was getting several e-mails per week.

About a year after the conference, I was curious about some of the people I had met: Brenda Star, whose galactic-themed website played Phil Collins's "In the Air Tonight"; Dr. Darcy, on whose website I took a quiz to find out if I was "ready for sex" (salient questions included "Can my partner and I 'legally' have sex?" and "Would I have sex if I weren't drunk or high?"); and Melissa, the first person I spoke to, who had no book or website or idea when last we spoke. I tried to contact them, one by one. Melissa was the only person who called me back. Were the rest all busy enjoying their newfound success? After the conference, Melissa told me, she had spent an additional $3,500 on a "market assessment." She admitted she was underwhelmed but blamed herself: "I think if I had already had a more defined presence, a specific website designed or something, it would have been more helpful." While she thought that the conference was too big—"you can't teach anything to six hundred people"—she was not regretful, explaining, "Had I never gotten on a plane and gone to Atlanta, I never would have gotten an idea on the way back. So something happened there; it stirred some intellectual creativity."

ME: So what's your book about?
MELISSA: I'm still trying to find a platform idea.
ME: How so?
M: Well, I didn't want to write a book unless [the market assessor] thought it was a good idea.
ME: Did she?

M: She thought I needed a more specific platform.

ME: [having no idea what "platform" means] What is your platform?

M: I'm trying to find a niche market, and then come up with a series.

ME: About . . . ?

M: I'm still refining the components I need.

ME: About . . . ?

M: What do you mean?

ME: I mean, generally, what's your subject matter? Like, what is it that you do?

M: Sending kids to college and paying for it.

ME: Jackpot!

M: Well . . . I had some universities who seemed interested, but then I found out schools don't have any money; they have no budget. That was annoying.

ME: That *is* annoying.

M: So now I'm going through a process of elimination, where I can get the highest dollar per effort hour.

ME: Huh. That's a stumper.

M: Yeah.

ME: Well, best of luck to you.

M: Best of luck to you. [pause] Uh, what is it that you do?

2

APPARENTLY, THERE ARE RULES

Control and the Defense Against Loss

Six months after my mother died in 1979, my paternal grandfather died. Eight months after that, my father remarried. His new wife legally adopted me. I was three years old. We were living in the same house that my father and biological mother had bought. Somewhat rashly, my father and new mother sold every single thing we owned, including the house, the furniture, and the car. This goes against conventional wisdom: according to self-help books on grieving children, preserving stability after a loss is paramount. Although I don't remember much about this time, I assume it must have been confusing; first my mother was replaced with another woman, and then we moved to another country. In pictures, I don't look like a particularly intelligent toddler—a boyfriend once pointed out that my mouth hangs open in almost every childhood photo—but I'm sure I suspected something was amiss.

We traveled around Europe. We went to Greece, Scotland,

Amsterdam, Italy. We lived in England for a few months, where I remember a delightful nanny named Cassandra who would tell me stories about King Arthur's court. In 1981, we finally settled in Paris. None of us spoke French. My father had become literally and figuratively untethered. He describes the year of his life when we traveled constantly as "the time when I had no keys." In Paris, there were keys, but everything else was strange. The only television show I recognized from home was *Zorro!* and the only word I recognized in it was also *Zorro,* and even that was rendered mysterious and unfamiliar when pronounced with a French accent. I remember feeling perpetually frightened and miserable. In most of the photographs from that time I am smiling and look cheerful; then again, in most of the photographs from that time I am holding an ice-cream cone.

The predicament of any child is a near-total lack of agency. Houses are bought and sold. Schools and clothes are picked out. Mysterious people come in and out of your house whom you have not invited. Dinner is served. You are not consulted. Depending on what kind of child you are, this can induce a feeling of freedom or anxiety (in yours truly, it was the latter).

Faced with an ever-changing landscape I became superstitious and ritualistic, mechanisms of perceived control. Life was something to be dominated, not experienced. When we left America, I brought a bag filled with Smurfs. The bag was plastic and shaped like a house. House things—windows and doors—were printed on the sides. The roof seam was a zipper where Smurfs could enter and exit. I loved that bag dearly. During our year of travel, when we arrived at whatever hotel room we were spending the night in, I would arrange the Smurfs *just so* on a shelf.

When I had nightmares, which was often, I rearranged all

of the objects in my room. If I had a good dream, nothing could change. I drew circles around objects before I moved them so I would know exactly where they went. Soon this obsessive habit extended to good days and bad days, good grades and bad grades, etc. To this day, when I am in a dark mood, it makes me feel better to rearrange the furniture.

I lived, as much as I could, in a fantasy world. I read constantly, avoiding contact with others, providing myself an escape into other lives, other places. I liked to sleep with books in my bed. My memories of books I read as a child are as real to me as my actual memories, and I have occasionally confused the two.

I was a hairbreadth shy of deranged. I loved fairy tales in which characters were turned to stone, and I used to pretend that my muscles and face were calcifying. I was practicing. I would stand in the same position as long as I could, or until I got bored. (If you ever wondered what only children do all day, it's stuff like this.) After I read *The Lion, the Witch, and the Wardrobe* I would step into every wardrobe I passed and look for the portal.

In a constant state of inventory, I would make lists of my stuffed animals, of my favorite books, of my friends. Perhaps it assuaged my anxiety around Things That Disappear. Lists give you the illusion that you can plan. Yet it is an illusion; nothing seems more superfluous than the grocery list of someone who has just been hit by a car. I say this as someone who has been hit by a car.

It is a basic unspoken assumption of every child that their parents are A) alive and B) going to stay that way for the foreseeable future. When I lost a parent I felt, deep down, that none of us was safe. So I created a world in which I ruled—it was a fantasy, but that didn't concern me. Instead of feeling powerless, I felt in control.

The world is chaos. Mothers die. Fathers marry stepmothers who don't like you. They move to France. They move back to America. Then they divorce, but because your stepmother adopted you she gets joint custody. In other words, your father gets to divorce her, but you don't. Later, as you age, you realize that this is not just the state of your household but the state of the world. Though you may exercise more control over your day-to-day life, the things we call our choices, there are always many more things that are out of your control, the least significant of which is the weather. Sometimes it is not just the outside world you can't control, but your inner world as well.

It's enough to drive anyone to the brink. One feels there has to be some order, even if it is self-imposed. Self-help is like a balm for this particular wound. Buying a book can make you feel better because it makes you feel like you are in control. I have started, it says. I am about to change something. It is said that many people buy self-help books and do not read them, or start to read them but do not finish them. (Most of the self-help books I bought for research were second-hand, and were heavily underlined and annotated for the first twenty pages.) Yet the temptation to buy these books remains, offering the illusory promise of structure in the face of chaos.

Imagine you are in crisis. You've just lost your job, or someone you loved. Imagine you have no idea how to proceed. You feel desperate. How much would you pay for something that would right your life? That would free you, for good, from your lesser self? How much would you pay just to feel that this was possible?

———

I would pay more than forty-five dollars, the fee for a workshop with the authors of *The Rules*, a self-help book on dating and marriage. *The Rules* was a hit when it appeared in 1995, selling over 3 million copies worldwide. The advice itself was even older; this book could have been written in the 1950s (the book's subtitle is *Time-tested Secrets for Capturing the Heart of Mr. Right*) or, for that matter, the 1850s. The authors embraced a traditional, old-fashioned outlook on male and female roles. In part due to the controversy over the seemingly out-of-date advice, the authors became celebrities overnight, and appeared on *Oprah*.

More than ten years later, *The Rules* had been supplanted by newer titles and was not nearly the monolith it used to be—and one of the coauthors had gotten divorced—but the book continued to have a dogged foothold. This was achieved partly through sequels: *The Rules II, The Rules for Marriage, The Rules for Online Dating, All the Rules, The Rules Dating Journal,* and *The Complete Book of Rules*. Additionally, an octopus-like apparatus with great suction had spread its tentacles through space and time into Rules support groups, Rules coaches, Rules facilitators in twenty-seven countries, and biannual seminars for the public, like this one, taught by the authors themselves. The repetition and multiplication of one concept is endemic in the world of self-help and the key to a certain level of profit.

In 2006 I signed up for the class, which promised to teach women the skills necessary for the acquisition of a husband. For only five extra dollars The Learning Annex offered to send me a course certificate, for which I could see no other use than an ironic fridge placement next to my strong-willed dog's also-ironic diploma from obedience school.

When I arrived at the Monday-night seminar unwashed, without makeup, in my favorite, dog-hair-covered green sweatpants, I was already breaking several Rules, namely:

"Look your best!"

"Don't aspire to the unisex look. Buy feminine-looking clothes . . . remember you're dressing for men. Don't leave the house without wearing makeup. Put lipstick on even when you go jogging."

The evening seminar was held at a high school near Madison Square Park. When I arrived I was instructed to wait in the lobby, a makeshift holding area for disparate Annex students waiting for their classroom assignments. I overheard several women gossiping about the Rules. "They've been on *Oprah,*" said a pretty woman with curly red hair, referring to the authors. "They're rich."

A desperate weather hung over this particular group of women, a group of which I was now a member. Regrettably, the person taking attendance was a man. I whispered that I was there for the Rules seminar and gave him my name to check off the list; he avoided eye contact.

Our classroom turned out to be a cafeteria with large, Reagan-era pictures of sandwiches on the walls. We sat in folding chairs facing a podium. Behind the podium, a large poster read in big, bold letters, ENTRÉES: FEED YOUR MIND, above which floated a picture of some harmful-looking rigatoni. Another picture featured a patty of unidentifiable origin, flanked by radioactively bright green and red peppers.

In New York City, prewar heating systems have only two settings: off and subtropical. The temperature in the classroom made me think of something my high school French teacher had told me about Sartre's play *No Exit*: when it was originally performed, the heat was slowly turned up in the theater during the performance, so that by the end the audience would feel like they were trapped in Hell. Fittingly, the exit from this classroom was behind the podium, making it impossible to sneak out unnoticed. Two women looking for seats joked about not being able to escape; I inserted myself into their conversation, trying to make friends. "You can leave whenever you want!" I said, too emphatically. They ignored me (see: sweatpants).

As the room filled up, to my surprise two men joined the class. One of them was a white man who was definitely in his seventies, if not his eighties. The other man was black, and probably in his forties. They did not appear to have come together. The old man scowled and looked irritated. He continually changed his mind about where to sit, as though he were playing a solo game of musical chairs. Since there were classes on other topics taking place in the building at the same time, I wondered if they were in the wrong room. Part of me was pleased: I was now no longer, as it were, the oddest man out.

Most of the women at the seminar were from New York and New Jersey, and they ranged in age from midtwenties to late fifties or early sixties. Not all of them were familiar with *The Rules*. "You're in for a treat!" one of the veterans exclaimed. Another woman shared that this was her third time at a Rules seminar. The women were mostly, but not entirely, white. A nice-looking older woman in a sharp business suit shared with her neighbor that she was "extremely successful in commercial real estate." Her neighbor said wistfully, "You must meet lots of men." The real-estate maven nodded, but imparted that "all the men I meet are already married." Several nearby women sighed theatrically.

The Rules is a book about dating and marriage, but it also appeals to our desire for control and stability. The built-in terror of any relationship is the potential for loss, and the secret dread lurking between the lines of relationship-advice books is the fear of dying alone. Any guilt one might feel over manipulating another person is easily disarmed by the fear of losing them.

Success can be achieved, self-help books tell us, by following a formula, like MVH's REAL WEALTH = IDEAS + ENERGY or Ben Franklin's charts. *The Rules* is another type of formula. This formula sets marriage as its goal, but the deeper appeal is the fantasy of omnipotence through controlling others. The book also prescribes a high level of self-control to one's diet, dress, conversational style, sexual behavior, and emotional self-regulation.

Self-help books for women have historically addressed relationships with others, primarily husbands and children. As women and men moved from a family-centered agrarian-based society to mixed industrial settings, they were confronted with an uncharted set of social rules, customs, and expectations. The Victorian era produced a formidable number of books on etiquette, or social rules, aiming to assuage the awkwardness of the unfamiliar, offering sage advice like "Never marry a rotter."

A person in the nineteenth century could easily learn new rules on subjects as varied as housewifery, proper rhetoric, manliness, gymnastics, cooking, how to be a lady, morals, and character, sometimes all in the same volume. In 1873 *Harper's Bazar* (now Bazaar) released a book for women called *The Bazar Book of Decorum: The Care of the Person, Manners, Etiquette, and Ceremonials*, which warned against misbehavior such as being the "social monster capable of asking twice for soup." Emily Post's *Etiquette* (1922) provided guidance on dressing babies for funerals, letter writing, hosting dinners with limited equipment, salutations, serving roast beef to guests (don't: it is a family dish), keeping a well-appointed house, accepting invitations, rejecting invitations, proper butler attire ("none but vulgarians would employ a butler [or any other house servant] who wears a mustache!"), allowing one's maids to receive "men friends," decencies of behavior, social climbing, proper use of a spoon, proper use of a fork, proper use of a knife, proper use of a fork and knife together, children at afternoon tea, and how to eat asparagus (don't let the juice run down your arm).

Post believed that, far from addressing trivial matters, proper etiquette was synonymous with good character. Good manners might not improve one's character, but character is not readily visible, and using the correct fork is. Self-help allows you to establish a custom or habit, practice it, perfect it, repeat it, and watch your reality change. Superficial skills translate seamlessly into a certain type of identity. Just as for existentialists, action is the only reality. A cruel act makes a cruel person.

George Washington, at age sixteen, hand copied a book called *Rules of Civility & Decent Behaviour In Company and Conversation*, both to learn said rules and to practice his penmanship. An etiquette book (rule #2: "When in Company, put not your Hands to any Part of the Body, not usualy [*sic*] Discovered."), it also covers philosophical and moral ground (rule #110: "Labour to keep alive in your Breast that Little Spark of Celestial fire Called Conscience."). While on the surface these types of books appear to be about manners and table settings, they are also about fitting in, social climbing, securing social position.

Learning certain precepts also promised women valuable security. The 1964 Nina Farewell book *Every Girl Is Entitled to a Husband* insists:

> Since [a husband] is so necessary an accessory, you cannot afford
> to give consideration to a man's wishes. Willy-nilly he must be
> hunted down, nudged into a favorable position, and then pres-
> sured, bribed, needled, wheedled, teased, trapped, or, if need be,

tricked, into delivering himself body and bankbook into your ever-lasting service. Your very life is at stake. Your social and economic status, your emotional well-being, your sexual salvation, your Motherhood potential—all are determined by marriage.

Although sentiments like "your very life is at stake" may seem extreme, there's a much greater precedent historically for the creation of a woman's identity (even, sometimes, the identity of the woman's entire family) through marriage than for the contemporary notions we have of marriage as an expression of love, partnership, and independent will. Many of these books see the ultimate role of a woman as mother, and assert the widely held belief that the only respectable path to motherhood is through marriage.

The book's chapters have titles like "Lures, Traps, Spells, For the Girl who wants a Man of Medicine or Man of Science," and "Kindness in Victory." Farewell frequently (and, it seems, appropriately) borrows from the idiom of business to relate her message to women, her favorite being the use of the pie chart (also an actual pie, also possibly the only pie in 1964 with the word "sex" on it) to detail what a woman can anticipate in a week of married life.

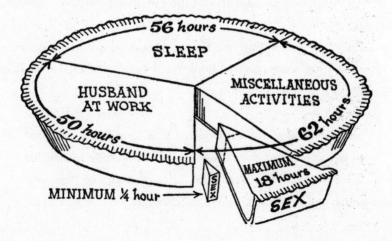

As expected, Farewell prizes marriage above all other options for women, perhaps because she considers marriage more of a social obligation than a personal fulfillment (although Farewell might argue that the two are synonymous). Farewell writes about romantic love as incidental to a successful marriage:

> This may be a shocking idea on first consideration. The very phrase, MARRIAGE WITHOUT LOVE has a disreputable look. Nevertheless, I am going to ask that every unmarried female read the following aloud: "I can marry without love." Do you find such a sentence difficult to voice? Force yourself. Now, say it over and over again. Observe how the shock value gradually diminishes. After a while, the words will drop from your lips as easily as How-do-you-do. What is more, you will come to believe in them.[*]

Farewell refers to her view of marriage as "civilized appeasement," and claims "the girl who feigns love for the man she marries is not a hypocrite but an integrated member of Society." Farewell's hard sell of married life suggests that her message might not have been self-evident, and this slight undercurrent of anxiety manifests in over-protesting statements like this: "the acquisition of a man is the worthiest ambition a girl can have."

Farewell's book resembles *The Rules* both in its ruthless attitude toward marriage and its assurance that wedded bliss can be attained through a specific program. It's worth noting that Farewell's book came out a year after *The Feminine Mystique* (1963), during a time when women's dependence on men was unpopular and considered retrograde. The popularity of books preaching exactly the opposite

---

[*]Go ahead, try it. It's creepy! It's fun! It's creepy-fun!

reminds us that the flip side of liberation is a loss of familiar structure. Being released from a traditional role can leave one with no
role, possibly a more frightening prospect. The prisoners miss the
prison because there they knew the rules.

———

We had been sitting for about fifteen minutes and our teachers had
not yet arrived. I was starting to feel faint from the heat, and to avoid
passing out had stripped down to an old undershirt. One woman
made a loud cell phone call and was vigorously shushed. After half
an hour of waiting amid rising temperatures, grumbling and irrita-
tion infested the room. An Amazon woman in a silver sequined top
and black leather miniskirt stood up and tried to assuage the restless
crowd. "I'm a certified Rules instructor," she announced in a high,
breathy affect, "and I'm happy to answer any questions while we
wait." She was greeted by stony silence and sat down nervously.

Ten minutes later, unhappiness escalating, the Amazon stood
again and said, "Don't worry. I have Sherrie's number. I'm going
to call her and see where she is." The fact that she had one of the
coauthor's phone numbers made her seem much more valuable,
and the women eyeballed her with vulpine interest. At that moment Sherrie Schneider walked through the door, wet and apolo-
getic and forty minutes late. Several women squealed. The old man
looked startled by the high-pitched noise.

Schneider was a slim, pretty woman in her forties with straight,
chocolate-colored hair snipped just past her shoulders. Before she
was a "Rules girl," Schneider was a gossip columnist for *Ad Week*. In
1996, *Entertainment Weekly* ran an article that contradicted her image
as a "neo–June Cleaver." Her former colleagues, including the au-

thor of the article, claimed that she directly contradicted rules like "don't reveal too much" by talking openly about her sex life.

"So sorry I'm late," Schneider said, putting down her Burberry umbrella and Burberry shopping bag, taking off her Burberry raincoat. "Ellen couldn't make it because she's sick." The room bloated with muted murmurs of disappointment. I was extremely disappointed because I had been looking forward to seeing Ellen Fein's teeth. Fein had infamously divorced several years before, and one of the causes for the divorce, I had read, was terribly botched dental work. The article, appearing in 2004 in Dublin's *Independent*, described the teeth:

> The bottom row of teeth is a pitiful sight—jagged, discolored and
> leaning back into her mouth. What looks like a large boil domi-
> nates her gum. . . . The top row is just strange—a row of extra-
> large white blocks that bear only a passing resemblance to teeth.

Although the "celebrity dentist" denied any liability, Fein was still engaged in a lawsuit against him, and had a link on the Rules website to baddentist.com, a website devoted to chronicling the dentist's alleged malpractice.

Schneider, meanwhile, had teeth nice enough to suggest that she could be related to a dental professional, and deployed them in a constant smile. She seemed genuinely thrilled to be leading the class, and faced us with a conspiratorial gleam in her eye.

"Okay," she said brightly, "who knows what the Rules are?"

Most of the women raised their hands. "Well, for those of you who don't know, they are a simple way of acting around men that can help any woman win the heart of the man of her dreams!" Schneider went on to explain that she and Fein wrote *The Rules* because "we knew so many women that were great and could not get a second date."

Schneider continued: "Both [Ellen and I] are naturally old-fashioned. I met my husband at a singles dance. It never works to approach a man. He has to walk over to you. Men are hunters and women cannot be. When you speak to a man first, it's over for him. You could be Elle Macpherson, but he'll dump you as soon as he meets his type. It is *completely* wrong to pursue a man."

The Rules makes certain assumptions about men (and women) that deny any agency to a woman who might be interested in something more than a one-night stand. Fein and Schneider acknowledge several times that their approach is self-abnegating, but ask you to ignore that because, hey, the Rules work (i.e., why don't you cuddle up with your self-worth in forty years when you are alone and living in an attic). According to the Rules, "Women who call men, ask them out . . . destroy male ambition and animal drive." The authors nod to your unshaven feminist skepticism, but insist that their approach is part of the natural order of the world:

> We understand why modern, career-oriented women have sometimes scoffed at our suggestions. They've been MBA-trained to "make things happen" and to take charge of their careers. However, a relationship with a man is different from a job. In a relationship, the man must take charge. He must propose. We are not making this up—biologically, he's the aggressor.*

Fein and Schneider make many small but helpful suggestions—

---

*Zsa Zsa Gabor contradicts this notion in her book *How to Catch a Man, How to Keep a Man, How to Get Rid of a Man* (1970). According to Zsa Zsa, who has been "consistently married since age 15 and a half," she "proposed to every one of [her] husbands."

express sympathy if his dog dies, the correct way to move hair out of your face, "sip, never slurp"—but overall they advocate a system best known as "playing hard to get."

The Rules can be broken down into several categories, among them, Never be sad:

Don't sound cynical or depressed . . . act as if you were born happy.

Be quiet:

Sometimes men just want to drive in silence without saying a word. Let them. Maybe he's thinking about how he's going to propose to you one day. Don't ruin his concentration.

Hide anything potentially undesirable (e.g., your mental illnesses and your copy of *The Rules*):

Before he comes to your apartment, tuck this book away in your top drawer and make sure any self-help books are out of sight. Have interesting or popular novels or nonfiction books in full view. Hide in the closet any grungy bathrobes or something you don't want him to see, such as a bottle of Prozac.

Pretend you are emotionally disinterested and preternaturally busy:

After seeing him once a week for the first month, you can see him twice or three times a week during the second month, and three to four times a week in the third month. But never more than four or five times a week unless you're engaged. Men must be conditioned to feel that if they want to see you seven days a week they have to marry you.

Fein and Schneider make some extremely counterintuitive suggestions: "It's good when men get upset; it means they care about you. If they're not angry, they're indifferent, and if they're indifferent, they've got one foot out the door." They also advise seeming sexually distant, not being sexually demanding or talking about "your needs" (unless he explicitly asks). Don't, under pain of death, mention the "M word" (marriage). And, of course, don't question the Rules: they make fun of other self-help books that contradict their advice, especially those containing the words "inner child."

The internecine snobberies of the self-help industry are rampant. The existence of a book must always be justified, and the easiest answer to why a self-help book is necessary is that the other ones aren't good enough. On some level this is just good business: my widget is better than his. Most philosophies are written in reaction to and to debunk what came before. The son kills the father. People who buy books on self-acceptance look down on people who buy books on getting married, and vice versa. We all have our own misery guilds.

Another rule states you should hide the Rules from your therapist. (I gleefully mentioned this rule to my usually laconic then-therapist, who was unable to hide the most withering look I have ever seen cross another human being's face.) Although I don't personally agree with many of these rules, the authors rebut with an argument I couldn't in good faith refute: "If you think you're too smart for the Rules, ask yourself, 'Am I married?'"

It is a long-standing convention of the self-help workshop that the leader invites a person who has benefited from their advice to provide a living, breathing inspirational story, anecdotal proof that the program works. They are the "after" to your "before." True to form, Schneider had invited one of her "success stories," a woman named Betsy, to substantiate the efficacy of the Rules. Betsy was in her thirties, had dyed-blond hair, and was from Long Island. Betsy opened by telling us, "I am the ultimate Rules girl because I got married twice in one year!" This tidbit was followed by gasps of delight. I was confused, because that didn't exactly seem the point. Ignoring this detail I settled into my chair, anticipating the simple pleasure of a narrative with a promised happy ending.

Before the Rules, Betsy explained, she'd had a series of bad relationships. "I wanted to get married more than anything. I would do whatever it took. I started consultations with Ellen and Sherrie. They're great with hair and makeup. They took me shopping. I came into Manhattan every single day to look for men."

Schneider added quickly, for those of us who might not look like Betsy, "Betsy didn't always look like this, you know. Ellen and I took her to the mall, we got her hair dyed, we showed her how to do her makeup."

Betsy blushed to the perimeter of her newly blond roots. If you like white spandex and sparkly sequins and pantsuits, you probably would have liked her outfit.

"Go on," Schneider urged, smiling.

Betsy continued, "He was a lawyer, he was nice-looking. I knew I wanted to marry him . . . It was hard for me not to call him," she said. "Instead I called Ellen and Sherrie. Sometimes six times a day! Or at midnight on a Saturday night because I was so miserable.

"I only saw him once a week for the first month. It drove him nuts! Ellen and Sherrie wouldn't let me see him. *They fall in love with you when they don't see you.* I did that with the first husband. He proposed in five months. My mistake was that I did ninety-five percent [of the Rules]. Buyer beware—you want to get married so bad, you have a guy who will propose, you ignore stuff 'cause you want to get married so bad. He showed little anger issues, but I didn't pay attention.

"When I introduced [my fiancé] to my father, he wasn't interested. He drank too much. He had a lot of contempt for his family. Find out how he feels about his mother. That's how he'll treat you. During the engagement I saw problems. But I was planning the wedding so I didn't care. Sherrie and Ellen say, *Be light and breezy and fun. [Men] don't know you've been crying in the bathtub because you're not married.* So when I got the ring I was like, I'm done."

Then Betsy's face changed. The brightness left her eyes, a sign that a narrative storm system was moving in. I started to feel anxious for her, as though I were watching a woman in a horror movie decide to check out that noise in the basement. What was happening to my feel-good story? Don't go down those stairs!

"I was so caught up in it, I guess, that I didn't notice the warning signs. I was so happy. We had a huge wedding. My parents spent . . ." She trailed off.

"I had the worst wedding night ever. The wedding was the most gorgeous thing ever. I wanted to have pigs in a blanket, you know, at the reception. My cousin likes them." The women nodded and smiled, also liking the little wieners, or perhaps having wiener-loving cousins. "But [my husband] wanted it to be classy.

"So I called the caterer and said no pigs in a blanket. But I guess they served them anyway. 'Cause we were in the limo and my cousin drove us back to our hotel and says, 'I loved the pigs in a blanket!' and [my husband] went crazy. My husband freaked because I laughed. I'm laughing. 'It's my wedding night,' I said, 'we're not going to talk about hot dogs.'

"That made him angry. I was wrong. If he's upset about it, *I* should be. He blamed me for the hot dogs. That was the first time I saw him get really angry. I cried all night on our wedding night. It was the worst wedding night ever."

At this point in the story I was starting to feel unsettled and sad. Betsy looked sad. Schneider looked sad. This was not how the inspirational story was supposed to trend. I started to wonder why, exactly, Schneider had invited Betsy to the seminar. And then her story got worse.

"After the wedding I found out he had financial problems. He had bad ethics. He was involved in a hospital scam. He was the most difficult husband. I lived with him for six weeks. He was very verbally abusive. He would grab my arm and shake me. He wasn't physically abusive—yet.

"Sherrie helped me with the Rules for Marriage. *You just imitate their opinions*—if he hates the caterer, then you hate the caterer. So, I learned that. Sherrie and I tried to keep the faith. We did the Rules for Marriage on him. I did everything to try to save the marriage. I tried to reconcile. Sherrie said, *Don't show him you're crying because a man doesn't want to see you crying.* Ellen said, *Forget it.*"

Schneider interrupted her: "Okay. Let's move on. Things are better now, right?"

Betsy seemed confused, lost in her own story; but she smiled absently and obediently moved on. "When I decided to leave, I went right back to the Rules. I didn't sit around and feel sorry for myself. The weekend I left I went right out to a singles dance, and met my next husband!"

The nervous audience giggled, relieved. I, on the other hand, was reminded of the Biblical story of Job. As a test of Job's faith, God kills Job's wife and children, takes away his property, and kills a long list of his farm animals. When Job's faith endures, God rewards him by replacing his wife, giving him even more children and more animals, and doubling his property. Somehow, this has never struck me as a satisfying reward. God still killed Job's wife and children, and he didn't bring them back.

I found Betsy's success story incredibly disturbing. Rather than feeling reassured by the sloppily grafted happy ending, I was struck by the fact that following the Rules had led this woman to marry someone whom she didn't get to know and who subsequently abused her.

A woman raised her hand and said, "I'm dying to ask you a question, because it's such a *heartwarming* story. Are you happy now?"

"I'm getting to that," Betsy said, all smiles again. "I wasn't devastated to lose [my first husband], because I hated him. But I *was* devastated to be single. I went right back at it. I didn't waste any time. I was on JDate the week I left him. I would role-play with Ellen and Sherrie. They made me cancel Monday-night dates. They'd say, *You are not going on a Monday. What's that? Monday?*

"By Saturday [my new husband] was so excited you'd think he'd never seen a woman before. He proposed after seven dates. And he is so great. He treats me so well, he loves my family; it's like night and day. And I'm so happy now."

"That's great," said Schneider. "And you did the Rules again, right?"

"Oh, absolutely," said Betsy. "I never let him know I was interested. He thought I was seeing other people when I was sitting at home thinking about him!" She smiled. "And he proposed to me in two months! He said he couldn't live without me."

"That's what happens when you do the Rules," Schneider chimed in, gleeful.

"We just got married this morning at city hall!" Betsy shrieked, holding up her newly bejeweled ring finger. "My divorce just came through yesterday!"

The women all applauded, and Betsy applauded too. I applauded, even though, to the extent that I identified with Betsy as a fellow woman and human being, I found the act of applauding this particular scenario awkward and tinged with masochism. Betsy rose and waved good-bye to the hopefuls like a beauty queen.

"Good luck," she said empathetically. "I have to go meet [my husband] for dinner. He has no idea where I am. He's never even heard of the Rules."

Her final statement elicited laughter that was, by nature, somewhat sinister.

The flaw in promises of stability via tested formulas is that it's impossible to guarantee they will apply in all human situations. Zsa Zsa Gabor, though not the most self-evident relationship role model, nails this idea in *How to Catch a Man, How to Keep a Man, How to Get Rid of a Man* (1970):

> [A] problem you'll have when you read my advice is that you may get mixed up, because it's not always so logical and consistent. But then love is not logical and consistent. And *I'm* certainly not logical and consistent. So why should my advice be. If you want that kind of thinking, go to a computer. Computers are always logical and consistent, and you see how often they get proposed to.

Betsy's story runs contrary to one of the claims of *The Rules*, that "Abuse doesn't happen in a Rules relationship because when you play hard to get and he works like hell to get you, he thinks you're the most beautiful wonderful woman in the world, even if you're not. He treats you like a precious jewel." A built-in failure of self-help books is that they cannot account for human dissimilarities, irregularities, and emotional errata.

While *The Rules* averred it could "save you $125 an hour in therapy bills," it could cost you a lot more if you want consultations with Fein and Schneider. On their website, I found a description of their services.

- An evaluation of your dating history (i.e., rule-breaking patterns) in past and present relationships
- An analysis of childhood issues that may affect the kind of men (abusive, alcoholic, bad financially, dysfunctional, etc.) that you are attracting
- How to be a Creature Unlike Any Other (CUAO), i.e., have self-esteem and feel good about yourself, whether or not you are in a relationship
- Personal shopping and makeovers. Some women don't understand why they are not meeting or attracting the men they want. In some cases, the problem is not *The Rules*, but their appearance. Plus: advice on plastic surgery including nose jobs, breast implants, liposuction, and dentistry (the good and the bad, including www.baddentist.com)

One-hour phone consultations with Fein and Schneider are $350; half an hour is $250; or you can e-mail them one question for $150.

They offer an e-mail course on the Rules (they claim some of the Rules are "difficult to grasp") for $800. I e-mailed Fein and Schneider to tell them I was writing a book about self-help. After ten questions, to which they gave answers so bland they're not worth repeating, they declined to answer any more:

> Hope this helps . . . good luck on your paper! We do get
> a lot of students and try to help, so hope this was, but
> any more questions we are going to have to charge you
> $50–$100 depending on how many questions as this also
> has become time consuming for us! Good luck!

Like most self-help magnates, Fein and Schneider created more than a series of books; they created a business. They train women to be "Rules facilitators" (which costs the women-in-training $1,200 for twelve one-hour sessions) and those women in turn charge other women for their Rules advice. The list of Rules facilitators on their website was more than a hundred names long, with women in over twenty countries. (In fact, at least five of the twenty-five or so women at the seminar were Rules facilitators.) One facilitator had even capitalized with her own book, called *How to Be a Rules Facilitator in Japan.*

Successful self-help empires create their own economies, which could be described as either trickle-down or Ponzi schemes. This system reminded me of a scene from Walt Disney's *Fantasia,* the only scene I remembered, probably because it made me so anxious. Mickey, in a sorcerer's hat, tries to attack a magic chair (it was threatening). He strikes it with an ax and cuts it in two. Now there are two magic chairs. He strikes them both with an ax and there are four! This chairs splitting and multiplying goes on until there are at least fifty dancing chairs, and it doesn't look good for Mickey. When I think about the fact that people pay money for expertise that they turn around and charge other people for, and so on and so on, it gives me a feeling similar to watching the menacing, prancing chairs: I feel slightly crazed, something akin to a light panic. They're *everywhere.**

Some of the Rules spin-offs were more bewildering than others. Dr. Tish, a Rules coach in Las Vegas, Nevada, combined psychic readings with the Rules. Dr. Tish's fee for a Rules reading was $95. You could also ask Dr. Tish to channel messages from your "own personal private Guardian Angel" or contact "loved ones on the other side." Ellen, the Amazon from the seminar, advertised herself as a Rules coach and energy healer, explaining, "Once you clear out the bad energy it's easy to find love."

After Betsy's departure, Schneider announced that for the last two hours she would answer questions. I cringed upon realizing that there were still two hours left. A wave of sleepiness swept across my brain, threatening to capsize intelligent thought. A middle-aged woman described an encounter with a man she had met by an elevator; after a few minutes of flirtation he had given her his business card. She liked him; he liked her; could she call him and ask him out?

"You can't call him," said Schneider flatly.

"But he doesn't have my number."

Schneider shrugged. "It won't work if you pursue him. He doesn't know your last name? He can't look you up?"

---

*My editor thinks I am remembering it wrong, that it was a broom, instead, which Mickey bewitches to carry pails of water to fill a pool in the sorcerer's chambers, but then he can't figure out how to make it stop, and the room becomes increasingly flooded. She's probably right. Still anxious-making.

"No," said the woman, disconsolate.

"Too bad," said Schneider. "I mean, you can call him if you want, but I'm telling you right now it's not going to work out."

The woman looked despairingly at her lap.

A very pretty twenty-four-year-old asked why her boyfriend hadn't yet said he loved her.

"How long have you been dating?" Schneider inquired.

"Four months."

"Has he given you any jewelry?"

"He's given me chocolate."

"He hasn't given you jewelry?"

"No."

"Not even on Valentine's Day?"

"He cooked me dinner."

"I wonder what you're doing that he hasn't said it."

"She hasn't slept with him!" the girl's friend gleefully chimed in.

"You want to marry him?" asked Schneider.

"Yes."

"The stricter you are, the sooner he'll say, 'I love you.' I would try pulling back a little."

"She's waiting for the 'I love you' to sleep with him. He's not trying," injected the friend.

"Well," said Schneider gravely, as though pronouncing the elegy for their relationship, "by your birthday you should get jewelry and 'I love you.' By the three-month mark they usually say it."

The friend then asked about her own relationship, saying how great it was that she and her boyfriend talked on the phone every day.

Schneider sharply disapproved. "I don't tolerate conversation. Only on the date. What do you do?"

"I'm a journalist," said the girl.

"You disappear between dates. You're busy. You're not in a relationship."

The journalist looked sad.

"You want a man to be obsessed with you?" asked Schneider. "Marry you? Disappear between dates."

The journalist looked super sad.

Schneider explained, turning now to all of us. "When I was dating my husband he couldn't talk to me more than five minutes a day. Now he can call me twelve times a day. But he gave me rings, he bought me a house; he owns me now, so it's okay."

Another girl raised her hand and shared she'd been on match.com for three years, but still didn't have a boyfriend. "I've been on fifty or sixty first dates! Can I ever contact someone myself?"

The very suggestion of going on fifty or sixty or even five first dates exhausted me. I could have fallen asleep just thinking about it. Also, did Sherrie Schneider really say, "He owns me now?"

"No," said Schneider firmly. "Well, you're a very pretty girl, so I'm not sure what you're doing wrong."

"Thank you!" said the girl, beaming.

After the promised two hours of Q and A, where each woman had a chance to sift through the minutiae of her dating behavior, Schneider ended the class. Many of the women were reluctant to leave, but Schneider assured them they could contact her via e-mail. Of the two male attendees, the younger man had left about an hour into the seminar, but the old man, still scowly and irritated, made his way slowly toward the door. I ran after him and trapped him in the stairwell. He eyed me suspiciously—and somewhat legitimately, after having listened for the past three hours to unscrupulous female schemes.

> Me: Can I ask you why you attended this class? Seeing
> as it seems exclusively geared toward women.
> Old Man: I just wanted to educate myself. It's a big
> world, and there's a lot to learn.
> Me: Did you learn anything here?
> OM: Absolutely.
> Me: What do you think of the advice they're giving,
> from a man's point of view?
> OM: They're right. Men don't want to get married.
> Sometimes we do need to be told what to do.
> Me: Really? You don't mind the strategizing, the dishonesty? You don't think it's manipulative?
> OM: No.

We walked outside, and I held the door for him. He smiled at me and opened his umbrella, even though the rain had stopped.

———

Not long after the Rules seminar, my father told me the following story.

Back in Paris in 1981, neither my father nor his new wife had a job. Once we left the United States, we had been living off the proceeds of the sale of our former life, money that lasted exactly two years. Then we were out of funds. New mother started taking

French lessons, and then embarked on an affair with her French teacher's husband. My father and new mother's marriage deteriorated. My father had survived the death of his wife and his father, all while caring for a two-year-old; he had tried to start over, and now everything was falling apart again. Confused and depressed, my father took a short trip to England, where he met up with his mother and brother. Out for a walk, they happened to pass a toy store. In the window was a play hospital.

The toy was a diorama of a hospital room, with four plastic beds fitted with plastic sheets, plastic patients, and plastic nurses. Tiny medical equipment hung from plastic carts; tiny charts hung from the feet of the plastic beds. Everything was clean and orderly. My dad looked into the window of the toy store, into the hospital diorama, at the white beds and the nurses with their white hats, yellow helmet hair, circular eyes, and one-line mouths imprinted into black, ever-persisting smiles.

It was safe in there; it was peaceful.

He wanted to be in that hospital room, to be taken care of by those nurses. He bought the play hospital, and took it back to his hotel.

He set up the hospital on a table in his room. He set the beds next to the charts, and the nurses next to the beds. He put the patients in the beds so the nurses could care for them. He played with the hospital for forty-five minutes, wishing himself inside. "I had a whole fantasy in my head. It was a mental hospital, and there was this one nurse," he told me, trailing off, comforted, for a moment, by a thirty-year-old fantasy. "The nurse," he said, referring to a tiny plastic figure built without much regard for verisimilitude, "was kind. It seemed like a place I wanted to be."

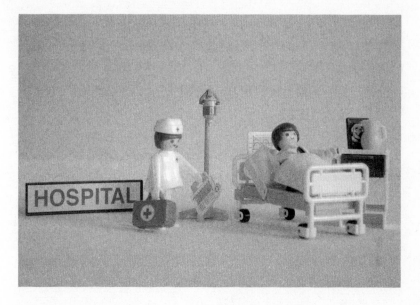

Looking into that play hospital and imagining himself there was a placebo; a viable, if temporary, sleight of hand. My father had taken an entropic situation and turned it into something he could control. The tiny figures could not die, cheat, or betray; they were his to manage.

"I felt better," he said. "It was a moment of epiphany. That was when I realized that toys could help people."

This image of my father was a difficult one for me to feel good about. He had chosen plastic people over real people. If mindfulness is the practice of inhabiting the present moment, this was the opposite of mindfulness. Instead, he used the mind as a means to escape. He refused to confront sorrow, substituting the imagination, a fantasy. Certainly I recognized this from my own life; my play hospital came in book form. But is this really a portrait of effective and felicitous self-help?

Self-help's rules can be comforting. They promise us control, a defense against loss. Even self-help's inherent isolation sidesteps potential rejection. The best thing about self-help is that it frees you from needing other people; the worst thing about self-help is exactly the same.

3

IN WHICH I WALK ON HOT COALS

The Power of Positive Thinking

My father claims to have been shy in his youth, but as a parent he was far from inconspicuous. He always drove a bright red convertible. He looked like Geraldo Rivera. If asked, he claimed to be Geraldo's better-looking brother. Entire school buses of children would shout "Geraldo! Geraldo!" as he waved at them from our car. He thought it was funny to pay highway tolls wearing a hand-puppet. With one exception toll workers did not find this amusing. They mostly seemed alarmed. Yet my father persisted. He once showed up at my school in a full gorilla costume (you might wonder how I knew that a man in a full gorilla costume was my father; the first clue was that my father *owned* a gorilla suit). Whenever he dropped me off at school he would shout as I sprinted from the car, "Today is the first day of the rest of your life!" (If my father asked me "What is today?" the correct answer was always "The first day of the rest of my life.")

For reasons unclear, my dad has always been fond of smuggling random inspirational expostulations, some murkier than others, into our father-daughter interactions. Another of his favorite phrases was "Go to the place where there is no time!" Whenever I asked him for anything, his response was always "Can do!" Sometimes he randomly yelled, "Hoppy Taw!" Hoppy Taw was the name of a Silly Putty–like product he had rejected from an inventor but whose name continued to delight him for many years. "Hoppy Taw" was an exclamation that could mean many things: my father could be referring to himself (I think the logic here was that Hoppy sounded like Poppy or Papi), indicating agreement, or just punctuating a conversation the way other people say "uh-huh." I suspect he said it even when no one else was around, just to mark his continued presence in the world.

His goofiness and sense of humor were part of his positive attitude; his jokes formed part of his defense against the hardness of life. Despite the fact that within five years my mother had died and his second marriage had ended in divorce and bad blood, he stared down a world of death and abandonment and betrayal and turned it into a world of gorilla costumes and hand puppets. It was his version of the American archetype of strength in the face of suffering, his Horatio Alger act. It was an ambitious, if untenable, illusionist feat.

Positive thinking has been a mainstay of self-help for hundreds of years. Thomas Jefferson wrote, "Nothing can stop the man with the right mental attitude from achieving his goal; nothing on earth can help the man with the wrong mental attitude." A hundred years later, Henry David Thoreau said, "Thought is the sculptor who can create the person you want to be." William James claimed that the greatest discovery of his generation was that "human beings can alter their lives by altering their attitudes of mind."

In the latter half of the nineteenth century, a man named Phineas P. Quimby founded the New Thought movement. Born in 1802, Quimby was a small, black-eyed, energetic man with little formal education. A clockmaker's apprentice, he abruptly changed careers in 1838 when he became fascinated with Mesmerism (named after Dr. Mesmer, who had attempted to cure illness using the mind, eliciting ridicule and rejection among his colleagues and eventually forcing him to leave Vienna in 1777). After practicing on a seventeen-year-old boy, Quimby proclaimed himself a healer, based only on his self-training. Quimby believed that disease was nothing more than an "error of the mind." Since disease sprang from the mind, not the body, it had to be cured using the mind.

He called illness "a deception, started like all other stories without any foundation, and handed down from generation to generation till the people believe it, and it has become a part of their lives." Even children were deceived by sickness. Explaining Quimby's methods, a Bangor, Maine, paper wrote in 1857, "In the case of a young child one might say, 'Surely here the mind can have nothing to do with the disease.' But not so. If a child coughs, the mind is cognizant of it, and dreads it, as he would dread the fire that has just burned him; and that dread increases the tendency to cough, and thus the disease is produced."

The upside of this theory was that disease was now easy for Quimby to cure. He would "simply converse with [the patient], and explain the causes of the troubles, and thus change the mind of the patient, and disabuse it of its errors and establish the truth in its place, which, if done, was the cure." He called this process "the Truth." Quimby described his method of cure in detail, referring to himself for some reason in the third person, as a doctor, and notably enamored of the recently introduced technology of the daguerreotype (which, one biography claims, he helped invent):*

> A patient comes to see Dr. Quimby. He renders himself absent to everything but the impression of the person's feelings. They are quickly daguerreotyped on him. They contain no intelligence, but shadow forth a reflection of themselves which he looks at. This contains the disease as it appears to the patient. Being confident that it is the shadow of a false idea, he is not afraid of it. . . . Then his feelings in regard to the disease, which are health and strength, are daguerreotyped onto the receptive plate of the patient, which also throws forth a shadow. The patient, seeing his shadow of the disease in a new light, gains confidence. This change of feeling is daguerreotyped onto the doctor again. This also throws forth a shadow. . . .

This back-and-forth daguerreotyping and shadow-throwing goes on way past the point of reader tolerance, until "the light takes its place, and there is nothing left of the disease."

Like any forward thinker, Quimby had detractors. One patient wrote that he was vilified for his ideas and "frequently threatened

---

*He also claimed to have invented the circular saw.

with mob violence." Still, he had myriad acolytes. Mary Baker Eddy, founder of the Christian Science movement, was one of his students. An 1860 article in the Lebanon, New Hampshire, *Free Press* declared that "his curing disease is perfectly intelligent and is in itself a new philosophy of life." Another article, written by a patient, defends him by contextualizing the resistance to his unorthodox methodology: "It is an ancient and time-honored custom for the educated classes to oppose every new thing that they cannot comprehend and account for."

Quimby treated over twelve thousand people using what he came to call the "Quimby method." He evidently thought quite highly of his contributions to humanity, so much so that he made the following cringe-worthy claim in November 1861: "I am a white abolitionist. The blacks, it is true, are slaves; but their slavery is a blessing, compared with that of the sick. I have seen many a white slave that would change places with the black. The only difference is that white slavery is sanctioned by public opinion." However deluded he may have been, Quimby laid the foundation for the belief that mental power could conquer disease, habit, and any obstacle life could conjure. His theories soon enthralled the cultural imagination.

In 1894, the first New Thought conference was held; in 1908 the National New Thought Alliance was formed. The New Thought movement was partial to what they called "mottoes." Henry Wood, a popular New Thought author, encouraged using mottoes such as "Divine Love fills Me," and "I am not Body." He advocated beholding words with the "mind's eye," thereby "telegraphing" thoughts into one's consciousness. Ralph Waldo Trine, one of the founders of the New Thought movement, wrote a best-selling book called

In Tune with the Infinite, which offered "suggestions" for thoughts to hold in one's mind, like "Dear everybody, I love you." He was read by Queen Victoria and Henry Ford, who directly attributed his success to Trine's book.

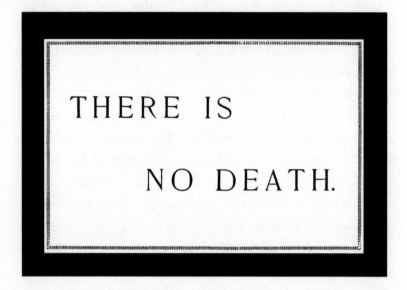

The power of positive thinking was even advertised to the younger set. In 1906, a story called "Thinking One Can" appeared in a youth magazine. After larger engines refuse to pull a train over a difficult hill, citing impossible conditions, a smaller engine volunteers. Even though it seems dubious for a little engine to accomplish what larger engines cannot, the smaller engine succeeds in pulling the train over the hill, while chanting, "I think I can, I think I can, I think I can." In 1930, the story reappeared with the title it still bears today: *The Little Engine That Could*. When we read this story to children, we teach them that positive thinking makes the impossible possible. The plot of the little engine is not inherently compelling or timeless; what has made this story endure for over a hundred years is its reinforcement of ⌐ valued cultural beliefs.

In 1922, a Frenchman named Emile Coué introduced America to Couéism, or autosuggestion. Like Quimby, Coué believed that a regimen of self-hypnosis through affirmations could cure ailments by replacing "thoughts of ailment" with "thoughts of cure." His book, *Self Mastery Through Conscious Autosuggestion*, was an immediate best seller. Coué coined what became a famous affirmation: "Day by day in every way I'm getting better and better."

Born in 1898, Norman Vincent Peale developed his theory of positive thinking to overcome his "inferiority complex." The pastor of the Marble Collegiate Church in New York City, Peale created the secular *Guideposts* magazine in 1945 as a forum for inspirational stories. He positioned himself at the intersection of religion and self-help, which magnified his message to a broader audience. When *The Power of Positive Thinking* came out in 1952 it stayed on the best-seller list for one hundred and eighty-six consecutive weeks. In *The Power of Positive Thinking* Peale urges the reader to "become a possibilitarian." Regardless of how hopeless and dark things may seem, you should always keep a positive attitude. You should always imagine yourself succeeding. "Do not develop obstacles in your imagination," he warns. Despite criticism from the psychological community, including the psychoanalyst with whom he had developed his theories, he had a weekly radio show called *The Art of Living*, which ran for fifty-four years. Ronald Reagan awarded him the Presidential Medal of Freedom in 1984.

One August night, a hundred teenagers and I stood in front of a giant bonfire, waiting to walk on hot coals. The weather was unusually cool, but it was hot near the fire. Kids joked around and pushed each other, but also seemed scared.

One kid to another: "It's like a meditation thing, right?"

Second kid, reassuring: "Yeah. It's all in your mind." He paused to reconsider. "But you should walk briskly."

I'd arrived at the Omega Teen Camp a few hours earlier. The camp was owned and operated by the Omega Institute in Rhinebeck, New York. Well-known in self-improvement circles, the Omega Institute's class topics range from practical (dealing with fear) to aspirational (personal growth) to just screwy (tree whispering). The teen camp aims to provide Omega *fils* with the self-empowerment they have provided to Omega *père* (upper-middle-class white folks, primarily) since 1977.

The camp was in Holmes, New York, a quiet, verdant small town with a dearth of road signage. Nancy, a tall and muscular woman, tended the fire, her brown hair pulled back into a ponytail. She had tanned, rough skin, the kind you get from being outdoors all of the time, or from leaning over fire on a regular basis. She wore a baseball hat with flames on the side. Her face was blackened like a chimney sweep's, and she wore heavy fire-retardant gloves. She carried a steel rake, and every few minutes she refreshed the coals by raking them out of the still-burning fire, as she muttered to herself, "It's not as big as I would have liked."

Nancy yelled at the restless crowd, "Be quiet!" The teenagers, who seemed to vacillate between periods of extreme lassitude and hyperactivity and were currently in hyperactive overdrive, resisted. "Come on, you guys," Nancy said, "we really have to try to keep the space sacred." She asked people who weren't going to participate to go to the other side of the field, and reminded us that if we'd recently had a stroke or were diabetic, we should not fire walk. Also, she reminded us to take off our toe jewelry.

"A lot of people ask me, *Am I going to burn myself?*" said Nancy to the large assembly. "We don't get *burnt*. We get *kissed*. We get *blessed*, as a reminder of what your intention is and what you have to do. When you get up here, stand in front of the fire. Pray. Intend. Open your heart. Walk straight across with a flat foot." She demonstrated a brisk but calm walk. "Don't hop all funny. Don't run. Anybody with a stroke or who has difficulty walking please do not do this. Let's sing."

The campers and counselors started to sing a tuneless song:

Earth my body,
Water my blood,
Enter my breath,
And fire my spirit.

They sang this eerie dirge over and over as Nancy spread the coals. The sky grew dark, darker. I started to get chills.

Ritual fire walking dates back to 1200 BC. In the 1930s, the phenomenon was studied at London's National Laboratory of Psychical Research, led by Harry Price, who made a study and a career out of exposing fraudulent mystical practices. Price rose to fame when he exposed William Hope's spirit photographs as hoaxes, and conducted a "black magic" experiment in which he tried to change a goat into a young man (it didn't work). In observing fire walking firsthand, Price set out to answer a number of questions, among them: "Is fire walking based on trickery? Can anyone do it? Do the performers prepare their feet? Can they convey their alleged immunity from burns to other persons? Does one have to be in an ecstatic or exalted position?"

The secret of fire walking turned out to be simple physics. Wood has low conductivity. Ash's insulating capabilities and a quick pace would keep anyone from getting burned. As University of Pittsburgh physics instructor David G. Willey told me unequivocally, "You can put your hand on very, very hot coals without burning."

Adam Simon, the camp director, was a balding, long-faced man in his fifties, with salt-and-pepper hair. Simon, who had dark eyes and a kind expression, exuded an ossified happiness one often encounters among the spiritually enlightened. He gently touched my shoulder and asked me if I was going to fire walk, adding, "The worst that can happen is a few little burns on your feet. Like if you held a match to your foot."

I tried to arrange my features in what I thought would read as a thoughtful, sincere, fire-walk-contemplating expression. In truth, I had no intention whatsoever of walking on hot coals. My intellectual inclination to be brave and my social desire to be accepted were in every way trumped by what I considered to be a reasonable and evolutionarily sound fear of setting my feet aflame.

The peacocking males were gamely attempting to infuse this spiritual ritual with sexual overtones. One of the boys bragged, "I prefer to walk [on the coals] more slowly because it's more spiritual." Some of them had their shirts off. I contemplated the fact that this camp had cost their parents several thousand dollars.

As we waited for the fire to die into hot coals, I tried to interview some of the teens, who were more interested in making out with each other. Teenage bodies agglomerated like rows of barnacles. After being ignored by at least thirty sullen campers, I found two girls kind enough to answer my questions. Earlier, they explained, there had been a ceremony for lighting the fire. The girls spoke in a patois of heartfelt nonsense; something about how one sets an "intention" to walk across the fire, that said intention is about confronting your fear and finding your power, and that you must keep that intention in your heart.

"What is an intention?"

An intention, they said, almost in unison, was something like a mantra. "For instance," explained one girl, "last year my intention was *I am beautiful*. I repeated that as I walked the fire. You step into a new life. You set a new intention for how to live. You feel stronger."

"And you didn't get hurt?"

"No. It felt like walking on a cloud. Or on warm sand."

I was highly skeptical, and it must have come across on my face, because the other girl said, "Sometimes you get a fire kiss," citing the camp's sweet neologism for a burned foot, an impressive bit of linguistic legerdemain.

"If you don't have an intention you shouldn't do it," said the first girl, and they both nodded with intense gravity.

Three boys beat bongo drums by the side of the fire, creating a restive atmosphere. The teens sang their fire song with gusto, reminding me too much of *Lord of the Flies*. Finally Nancy interrupted the song and said, "Come on, whoever wants to walk." They ran excitedly toward the fire in a chaotic, safety-blind fashion. "Single-file line!" shouted a female counselor with stringy blond hair, face paint, and a pierced belly button.

The kids grumbled but reluctantly organized themselves into an approximate queue. They began to walk across the coals: one at a time, over a glowing bed of embers five feet wide and eight feet long, or about three strides. There were still flames shooting from the coals. I was impressed. Some kids in line didn't seem so focused. They horsed around, shoving each other, teasing, "What's *your* intention?" But when they got close to the fire they shut up fast.

There was drumming, clapping, ululation. Each kid walked across the coals to shouts of encouragement and into the arms of two teenage girls who had formed a self-appointed reception line of hugs. (The teenage boys appeared especially psyched about this.) It was an opportunity for peer validation, which most teens don't see the likes of in high school, and which really cannot be overestimated. They were so happy, so proud, so accepted, so close to female breasts. Fire walking was turning out to be a powerful anodyne for the particular malaise, insecurity, and disenfranchised suffering that attends being teenaged. It was surprisingly moving to me because it meant so much to them.

The campers walked on coals, several times over. As soon as they finished, they eagerly hopped back on the end of the line. I saw only one kid even hesitate. It was pitch-dark now, and the coals were glowing a deeper, more fiery red. Toward the end of the ceremony, I reluctantly joined the line. Anxiety pounded in my stomach. With only three people ahead of me, Nancy stopped the line and raked on fresh hot coals.

I was having difficulty breathing normally. Adrenaline filled my body, pricking my arms and legs with thousands of tiny, invisible needles.

The person in front of me walked on the coals. I was next.

Despite my visceral fear, science won in the end. Walking on the coals didn't hurt at all. It did feel like walking on warm sand. I was deeply relieved, and admittedly self-congratulatory. I doubt I'll become a bungee jumper anytime soon, but I did glimpse the intense and pleasurable relief that follows an adrenaline-fueled fear.

Nancy drew the ceremony to a close. As she put out the fire she said, "It is not our deepest fear that we are inadequate. Our deepest fear is that we are powerful beyond limitation." I pondered her words. Was that true? Did I have any idea what she was talking about? Was there even any difference between her two sentences, practically speaking?

She said, calmly, with conviction, "Your purpose on earth is to reveal the glory of God, or Allah, or whoever you pray to."

The night was over. It was so dark I couldn't see my feet. I wiped my runny nose with a sock. Nancy said, "Show the world your light." The teens cheered and clapped and I thought I heard someone clanging a cowbell.

My father has always faced challenges with a blend of optimism and silliness that often involved writing songs about problems instead of facing them. As a child, I found this pleasing. When my malevolent stepbrother, a teenager so angry he always seemed one tantrum away from a manslaughter charge, tormented the household with his moods, my father made up a song. I don't remember how it went; only that we used to sing it in the car with gusto. When he and my current stepmother (mother #3, if you're keeping count) had problems, he made up the song "Leavin' Love Alone." This one I do remember some lyrics to, probably because I learned to play it on the piano, where we would sing it when she wasn't home. It had a bluesy, mournful tone:

I'm packing my bags
I'm leaving today

If the postman tries to find me
Tell him I moved far away

I'm going to New Orleans
It's the city of music and dreams
I'll drown my sorrow in a bottle of beer
And a plate of catfish and beans

'Cause I'm leavin', I'm leavin' love alone . . .

My father neither packed his bags nor drowned his sorrows in a plate of catfish and beans, but these little alternate universes, simple and ridiculous, floated over the landscape, keeping us entertained and distracted. They also kept us permanently stranded in the very situations they temporarily helped us escape. Positive thinking can look an awful lot like old-fashioned denial. What we called optimism often caused a kind of cognitive dissonance I later came to call "the fog." Being in the fog felt like that last moment of consciousness before you fall asleep. You are just on the verge of seeing something, but then it disappears and you forget it. The fog protected me from seeing that our attitudes didn't always reflect our reality. Just when I was on the verge of anger or sadness, the fog washed over me until I felt light and pleasantly confused.

Ultimately, affirmations and believing in the power of one's mind should be used as only part of an arsenal of tools against despair, an arsenal that includes admitting despair. Recently, I asked my dad why he had been so relentlessly positive in my younger years, and why he had constantly loaded even our most casual conversations with imperative affirmations. Did he really want me to consider that every day was the first day of the rest of my life, or was he just teasing me? He responded via e-mail,

> Hi friend,
> As corny as it was, I was trying to convey that you had
> the responsibility and the power to shape your own life.
> The context, of course, was that [my second wife, now ex]
> was acting crazy, the situation with [my third wife] was
> nuts. In other words, you were being buffeted around by a
> storm of neurotics, and I wasn't sure I was helping much.
> As you recall, I also like to repeat phrases over and over
> again, as did my Dad.
>
> Love,
> Your Dad

There are undeniable benefits to positive thinking—increased life span, decreased depression, less stress. It's even thought to stave off heart attacks and common colds. Sometimes the difference between the glass half-full or half-empty is a simple shift in perspective. Yet life is full of ups and downs, and there is something inhuman about addressing each obstacle with the same set of tools. Is there not value and even joy to be found in negative thinking, bitchy gossip, schadenfreude, aggression?

Considering the pleasures of negativity reminded me of a story a counselor at the Omega Teen Camp had told me. This counselor was in charge of the oldest boys, whom he described as "the ones who bring drugs and have sex." A particular camper had been breaking rules all summer, constantly challenging the counselor's authority. Finally, he'd had enough. The counselor knew that said teen had plans to sneak off into the woods after the counselors were asleep, so said counselor corralled other end-of-their-rope counselors and, after said teen pretended to go to sleep for the night, they set about creating the most giant and complicated booby trap, which involved items as varied as benches and tambourines, and which made the phrase "booby trap" seem particularly apt, given the circumstances.

They called it Operation Cock Block. "He stayed up until seven in the morning trying to figure out how to get out of the cabin," said the counselor, laughing, unable to conceal his glee. Then, maybe because he was so palpably pleased and I was a complete stranger, he amended, "Normally I wouldn't have cared that much, but this kid's been giving me trouble all session. I shouldn't say this, because the camp's about positivity—but his spirit was crushed and I was happy."

4

DR. CHOKING Game

The Cult of Expertise

CNN was on the phone. So was ABC, FOX News, and CNN (again). In 2006, after years of being largely ignored by the non-professional public, my father was suddenly invited on multiple television shows to give his expert opinion on the choking game. Ironically, the choking game was one thing my father, in his forty years of work in child psychology and parenting, had never heard of. I was standing in line at my local Mail Boxes Etc., when my cell phone rang.

> Dad: I have a question.
> Me: Shoot.
> Dad: Do you know what this choking game is?
> Me: What game?
> Dad: People choke themselves . . . ? Sometimes they ac-
>   cidentally die . . . ?

Me: [whispering] I think it's called autoerotic asphyxiation.

Dad: Auto what?

Me: [looking around nervously at the crowded Mail Boxes Etc., where people actually *know* me] It's a masturbating thing.

Dad: No, I don't think that's it.

Me: It is. People do it to, um, enhance their masturbation.

Dad: [suspicious] How do you know this?

Me: [innocently] Uh, I saw it on *Law and Order? SVU*, I think?

Dad: No, I think these kids just choke each other. There's no sexual component.

Me: [annoyed, raising my voice] There *is* a sexual component. It's for *masturbation!* That INXS guy died that way. I'm *telling* you.

Dad: No, I don't think so.

It turned out I was wrong. The game my father and I had never heard of had, apparently, been played by every single person I know. "Oh yeah, I played that," each confessed in turn. "I used to choke my little brother to make him pass out," said my ex-boyfriend, adding sweetly, "I guess I probably shouldn't have done that."

The choking game* refers to the practice of choking oneself,

---

*The CNN website reported that among the many aliases of the choking game are the "pass-out game," the "fainting game," the "tingling game," the "something dreaming game," and inexplicably, "space monkey."

or one's friends, in order to deprive the brain of oxygen. Insufficient oxygen to the brain produces a tingling sensation, a feeling of euphoria, or hallucinations. It's also dangerous, because when you pass out you can accidentally choke yourself to death. Although this "game" has been going on for quite some time (at least fifty years, by my ad hoc research), the media became newly interested in the summer of 2006. Some producer found my father's name, and invited him to give an expert opinion on their show. Once he gave one interview, he *was* the de facto choking game expert. Soon he was on a different show every week. I started to call him Dr. Choking Game, a name he did not relish. Yet the fact remained that when children choked themselves anywhere in America, his telephone rang.

———

The word "expert" entered the English language around 1825, coinciding with the Industrial Revolution. Knowledge was becoming more specialized; in an assembly line, for instance, one would be trained to do a specific task, and then hand off the product to another person with an equally isolated task, turning workers into specialists instead of generalists.

Within some fields there are rigorous criteria for expertise. Not anyone, thankfully, can perform brain surgery or fly a plane (although a popular magazine from the early twentieth century featured an article titled "I Had Appendicitis and Cured It Myself"). But within the field of self-help, there are almost no objective criteria. Some authors have advanced degrees or extensive training, and some have none. Phineas P. Quimby declared himself a doctor without receiving any formal medical degree. Some authors perform an act of self-fulfilling prophecy. Before Chicken Soup, Mark Victor Hansen was a businessman; afterward, he was an expert on self-help. Perhaps my favorite explanation of what makes an expert comes from Mark Twain: "an ordinary fellow from another town."

Some authors choose to address their lack of qualification directly. A book called *Quantum Wellness,* by Kathy Freston, begins, "When Harvey Weinstein first suggested that I write a book on wellness, I thought, 'Who am I to speak on such a broad and complex subject?' But respecting Harvey's instincts as I do . . ." Given that Freston's author photo shows a stunning, fit blonde, it does not take a gargantuan leap of imagination to wonder if Harvey Weinstein's support was not solely based on her ability to tackle "broad and complex" subjects. Now Freston is a *"New York Times* best-selling author" who has appeared on *Oprah* and *The Dr. Oz Show,* among others.

The very notion of expertise is dubious, as reflected by the disclaimer you will find in the front of almost every self-help book today (the disclaimer also reflects the fear of being sued). In minute print, publishers relate that the book contains "opinions and ideas" that are meant to be "helpful and informative" but *do not constitute professional advice.* At my local Barnes & Noble most of the books in the psychology section are self-help books written for laypeople. Most, but not all, are written by people with higher education credentials, a word whose root is *credo,* or belief. Yet we are still warned that the books should not be "relied upon" as method or diagnosis. Often the authors themselves will—and rightfully so—warn that just reading a book will not solve your problems. They say goal-reaching will take years of work and "nothing short of your total commitment." "There are no shortcuts," they advise. "This book is not intended as a substitute for treatment with a doctor or professional therapist," they insist. The careful reader also may encounter disclaimers like this: "Check with a physician or licensed sex therapist before attempting any sexual act that you are unfamiliar with."

Does anyone ever read these disclaimers? Like most people, I routinely toss privacy notices from my bank or scroll down and check "I agree" without a cursory glance. This often makes me feel anxious—what did I just agree to?—though not concerned enough to scroll through twenty pages of nanoscale, spirit-crushing fine print.

For authorities on parenting, the appearance of expertise is often buttressed by the fact that they have not only studied parenting, they *are* parents. Writers of self-help books routinely produce their own research—especially in the field of psychology—and if they are parents, they often experiment on their own children. They are, after all, *just sitting there*. When Darwin's first child, William Erasmus, was born on December 27, 1839, Darwin promptly got out a paper and pen: "I had excellent opportunities for close observation, and wrote down at once whatever was observed." As might be the argument of any of these experimenting parents, it was a crime of opportunity. Darwin reported that his son showed no aptitude for holding things, whereas his daughter was more "neat" and "efficient" in her pen and pencil holding. His son was, however, a gifted catapulter of many objects.

My father also tested his games on me. I remember the first time my dad tried to get me to play a cooperative game, which teaches teamwork instead of fostering competition.

Dad: Everyone has to finish the game, or no one wins.

Me: What?

Dad: No one wins unless everyone wins.

Me: So no one wins.

Dad: No, everyone wins.

The field of psychology is littered with experts who tested their theories on their unsuspecting offspring. Jean Piaget, the famous developmental psychologist, observed his own children to substantiate his theories. Clarence Leuba, another psychologist, would not allow his children to be tickled by anyone but him, while wearing a mask, in order to test whether a laughing response was innate or learned. Even this tickling was highly controlled, starting with light tickling, and moving to heavy tickling, while keeping separate notes on areas of the body. In 1933, Mrs. Leuba one day accidentally forgot protocol and bounced her son on her knee while herself laughing. Fearing his wife had contaminated the results, Leuba started over with his next child, a daughter.

Some parenting experts borrowed other people's children. In the early twentieth century, John B. Watson set out to discover whether fear, among other things, was learned or inherent. First, Watson placed his tiny subjects in a black-walled room without furniture. Infants were then presented potential fear stimuli, including a black cat ("reaching out to touch the cat's fur, eyes, and nose was the invariable response"); a rabbit ("catching the ears of the animal in one hand and attempting to put it in the mouth was one of the favorite responses"); a pigeon ("we have even had the pigeon moving and flapping its wings near the baby's face"); and fire ("the infant eagerly reached toward the flame and had to be restrained . . . as the fire became hot, reaching and manipulatory response died down"). In a famous experiment, Watson conditioned a nine-month-old to fear a white rat; every time "Little Albert" touched the rat, Watson banged a steel hammer behind the poor child's head.

Watson's 1924 best seller, *Behaviorism*, called parents "incompetent" and said they should be prosecuted for "psychological murder."* Watson believed you should not hug and kiss your children, but shake hands with them in the morning. He was also a proponent of "infant farms" and advocated a communal child-rearing environment where a child would be rotated among several sets of parents. Watson believed that parents had ultimate control, and responsibility, over how their children turned out. Of Watson's four children, one killed himself and another attempted suicide multiple times.

B. F. Skinner, a devotee of Watson and author of some parenting guides, described in a 1945 *Ladies' Home Journal* article a child-rearing tool he had invented and tested on his daughter. He called it "Baby in a Box." Since the enclosure was completely sanitary, Skinner explained with palpable self-satisfaction, his daughter never caught colds or other infections from the neighborhood children who "troop in to see her . . . and keep their school-age diseases to themselves." Only about fifty of the baby boxes were ever purchased. The baby box was never widely manufactured, though one businessman tried to manufacture it under the name Heir Conditioner. Despite this failure, in the 1950s the US Army funded Skinner's experiments to see if pigeons could control guided missiles.

Still, the prize for most atrocious behavior when using one's own children as guinea pigs would probably go to Dr. Moritz Schreber, a nineteenth-century German orthopedist who wrote eighteen popu-

---

*And not, puzzlingly, because some of them had allowed him to flap pigeon wings on their babies' faces.

lar books and booklets on the education of children. In *The Harmful Body Positions and Habits of Children, Including a Statement of Counteracting Measures* (1853), Dr. Schreber describes an invention of his called the *Schrebersche Geradehalter* (translation: Schreber's straight-holder), an iron device that forces children to sit up straight when they are seated, and a belt for proper posture while sleeping, which looks remarkably similar to the strapped restraints they use in mental institutions. His *Kopfhalter* was a "head-holder" used to prevent the child's head from falling sideways; it resembled an iron helmet with a chin strap. Dr. Schreber recommends withholding food if posture exercises are not performed, thereby "crushing" any disobedience. Dr. Schreber proudly acknowledged having used his methods on his own children.

His son, Daniel Schreber, was labeled a paranoid schizophrenic and institutionalized for most of his adult life. In 1900, Daniel began a journal about his time in the asylum, which was later published as *Memoirs of My Nervous Illness*. When Daniel's memoirs were studied by Freud, Freud concluded that the paranoia was brought on by a repressed homosexuality (he did like to dress in women's clothing and thought that his sex organs were changing from male to female, a process he called "unmanning"). In 1973, however, Dr. Morton Schatzman argued in his book *Soul Murder* that Daniel's "nervous illness" was likely a mental breakdown caused by his father's abusive parenting techniques.

John Locke, without whose "blank slate" theory parenting books might not exist, wrote his own parenting treatise in 1692, *Some Thoughts Concerning Education*. Though he never married or had children, Locke claimed that he was constantly asked for parenting advice. What seems to this reader an excessive amount of text is devoted to the subject of acclimatization; children should be exposed early to environmental dangers, Locke argues, so that they will be able to endure them later on. According to Locke, the greatest danger facing seventeenth-century youth was "rapid temperature change, such as running and being hot, and then sitting on the cold earth." However, the following advice just seems like a bad idea: "I will also advise his feet to be wash'd every day in cold water, and to have his shoes so thin, that they might leak and let in water." Locke warns that you should follow his advice, unless "you have a mind to make your children, when grown up, weary of you, and secretly to say within themselves, When will you die, father?"

For my father, being an expert on the choking game was a fast and loose business. Once he was called while on vacation at his sister-in-law's in Los Angeles. A producer from CNN informed him that a child had accidentally hanged himself in Sacramento. They asked if they could speedily send a camera crew to his sister-in-law's house. They also wanted to know if she had any rope.

"So you can show us how it happened," explained the producer, as though that were a normal request. My father refused.

"What if we bring a rope?" asked the producer.

"If I show kids how to hang themselves on TV," my father said, "they will go do it." The CNN producer seemed surprised by this notion.

"So . . . no rope?"

On another CNN show, an anchorman asked my father, in all seriousness, "Dr. Shapiro, should children hang themselves?"

"No," said my father, as though there were another possible answer. "They should not."

Finally the media seemed to lose interest. I think my father was mostly relieved. Despite his dream of having a more mainstream audience, he had always been ambivalent about these television segments on the choking game. On the one hand it was a public service of sorts; on the other hand, whenever one talked about the choking game, the incidences of it increased. It was impossible to weigh the benefit against the harm.

A few years passed. Then, in the spring of 2009, my father received a call from *The Dr. Oz Show*. Three months earlier, he was told, an eighteen-year-old in Florida had accidentally killed himself while hanging from a belt tied to a closet rod. The parents assumed it was suicide; they'd never heard of the choking game. Their son's sudden death was especially shocking and confusing to them since he'd left no note and hadn't seemed depressed. Their pediatrician alerted them to the possibility that their son had not intended to die, and when they learned about the choking game, they became convinced that this was his real cause of death. A close friend of the boy's confirmed they had played the choking game on several occasions. Would my father like to be on *The Dr. Oz Show* as their expert?

He sighed. "Sure."

Less than a week later, I met my father on a sunny day in front of 30 Rockefeller Plaza. After going through NBC security, we were escorted to a green room. The room was windowless and beige; the only decorations on the wall were three framed headshots of Dr. Oz, a man who bears some resemblance to an underfed werewolf. There was a worn couch and two chairs, upholstered in a hotel fabric so confused and ugly I wondered if it was intended as a theft deterrent. Two halogen lamps, leaning at

Tower of Pisa angles, dispatched uneven swaths of harsh light. A dropped ceiling of acoustic tiles hovered above a dirty navy carpet and a shiny black coffee table. A grass centerpiece sat on the coffee table with decapitated rose heads sitting on top of it, more pathetic than artistic. It was freezing cold, and I used my coat as a blanket. There was a TV, but we couldn't figure out how to turn it on. We had two hours to kill.

"Once I was in a green room with an old man, a monkey, and an accordion," said my father.

Today, because the other guests were the family and friends of the recently deceased teenager, we were not sharing a room, a fact I was grateful for. It was hard for me to understand why anyone who had suffered this kind of a loss would want to expose themselves on national television. I asked my dad what he thought might be their motivation.

"They feel very guilty," said my father. "They thought it was a suicide. Even the coroner had never heard of the choking game."

A gurney rolled by the green room, with a dummy on it, covered by a thin sheet. "I hope that's not a real body," joked my dad. "Or the last guest on the show." I rolled my eyes, but my father wasn't completely wrong. It turned out that, in a new twist on the usual choking game story, the show had decided to start the segment with a reenactment of an autopsy. A real medical examiner, Dr. G, who like Dr. Oz had her own eponymous TV show, was going to simulate the autopsy on a dummy. As reenactments go, it was firmly on the creepy side of an already creepy scale. Odder still, the dummy they were using was an old man, despite the fact that the choking game was played almost exclusively by teens and preteens. I wondered why they had made this unrealistic choice. I supposed they were squeamish about doing an autopsy of a plastic child on television; though, given that they were comfortable televising a recreated autopsy with some verisimilitude, it seemed like an arbitrary place to draw the line.

"Is the autopsy really necessary?" I asked my dad.

"I think Dr. Oz is smart and well-intentioned," said my dad. "But he still has to entertain."

Finally, the producer who had invited my dad to the show leaped into the room. He either existed in a constant state of natural enthusiasm, or he'd had way too much coffee. He spoke three times as fast as my father. The producer looked about twenty-five years old, and wore a maroon sweater and beige slacks.

"Dr. Shapiro!" he shouted with unfettered delight.

The producer explained to my father how the segment would run. First the autopsy. Then the family would speak ("Such a sad story," he said, seeming to mean it, while still projecting an unmistakable joie de vivre). Then, he explained, Dr. Oz would ask my dad a scripted question, after which Dr. Oz might ask unscripted questions.

"Would you like to rehearse now?" he asked my father.

"Great!" shouted the producer, answering his own question. He read from the segment script, pretending to be Dr. Oz, but without affect, a dramaturgical choice that gave his words an unexpected chill.

"AMERICA, I AM SOUNDING THE ALARM. AS A PARENT OR A GRANDPARENT YOU PROBABLY HAVEN'T HEARD OF IT, AND, CHANCES ARE, NEITHER HAS YOUR DOCTOR. IT'S A GAME YOUR CHILDREN COULD BE PLAYING UNDER YOUR ROOF, RIGHT NOW, WITH-

OUT YOUR KNOWLEDGE, AND IT COULD BE DEADLY. IT GOES BY MANY EXOTIC NAMES: RUSH, PURPLE DRAGON, SPACE MONKEY, FUNKY CHICKEN, CLOUD 9, BUT IT'S BEST KNOWN AS THE CHOKING GAME. IS *YOUR* CHILD PLAYING?"

The producer continued, himself again. "So then the family talks, et cetera, and then Dr. Oz will ask you, 'Dr. Shapiro, is the choking game as addictive as drugs or alcohol?'"

My dad was nonplussed. "Well, no," he said.

"What?" said the producer, again dropping the persona of Dr. Oz. "It's not?"

"No, not really," said my dad quietly. "The issue is more the availability. Kids who don't have access to drugs or alcohol can always play the choking game with their own body."

"But, I mean . . . can't it be . . . I mean, isn't any behavior addictive?" The producer frowned. "I'd like to start it a bit stronger. So you could say, 'Any behavior is addictive, you know, maybe not as strong as alcohol or drugs . . . '"

"But it *isn't* addictive, per se."

"Right," the producer said, his tone contradicting his agreement. "It isn't?"

"No, not per se."

"Right."

"Cutting and burning," explained my father, "that tends to be very addictive. The choking game, honestly, is not as addictive as drugs or alcohol. To me, the point is, it's just as dangerous. You only have to do it once and you could die. The addiction is not the issue, it's the danger."

"Hm. Okay. Well, I'm just trying to think of how we could

word it. Because what I don't want to say is, what I *don't* want to do is to say, 'No, it's not addictive.'"

Something about the way the producer couldn't give up on the addictive thing reminded me of a toddler trying to dislodge his giant head from a stair banister, unsuccessfully, while a bunch of grown-ups stand around anxiously.

"Why not ask me, 'Is it as dangerous as drugs or alcohol?'" said my father, applying some strategic Vaseline to the situation.

"But that's . . ." He paused, trying to process the suggestion. "It's not . . ." He tried again. "But would you agree that any behavior *can* be addictive?"

My father repeated the words slowly, as though he were considering them. "Any behavior—no, not any behavior can be addictive. It depends on the person. *You* might be more likely to be addicted to drugs or alcohol, but *I* might not be."

The more explosive the energy of the producer, the calmer my father seemed.

"Can we start it that way, maybe?" the young producer said. "It's a circumstantial situation, it depends on the person . . ."

"But this eighteen-year-old who died, he wasn't addicted, was he?"

"No! But we're not talking about him specifically."

With patience and the slightly condescending tone of a kindergarten teacher, my dad said, "Well, then we shouldn't mislead the public and say that. It's not that addictive. That's not the key issue. The key issue is that it's dangerous."

"So I'm just trying to think of how we could . . . I mean I want it to come across . . . I don't want to downsize it, that's my worry."

"Right. I understand. Well, why do you come back to that particular point?"

(This, by the way, is a classic psychologist move: asking why the question was asked, in order to evade the question.)

"'Cause, I'm thinking, it's like, it's interesting. People might be thinking, why are kids doing it? Are they doing it because it's addictive? Do they have no control over it?" Every time he asked a question, he spoke faster.

"No, that's not true," said my dad, amused. I tried not to laugh.

"Right, right, right," said the producer, the wheels of his brain spinning but failing to gain any traction.

"They do it because at that age they tend to experiment with their bodies, and they don't have the same judgment that you or I do."

"Mm-hm. So what . . . so how can we spin your answer, so that it's not . . . What if we say, 'Dr. Shapiro, is it as addictive as drugs or alcohol?' And you say, 'My main concern is that it's more dangerous than drugs or alcohol.'"

"Okay . . . Are you sure you don't want to change the question?"

Finally, the producer broke. "You know what? I'll change it," he said, giving up. "I'll change it to dangerous. It's just easier. Okay! You got me!" He laughed. He threw up his hands. My dad laughed. I, who had been suppressing laughter for about five minutes now, laughed so hard I almost fell off the arm of the sofa where I had been perched. We were all relieved.

"You're the producer," chuckled my dad, in a tone of you-know-best.

"But you should still mention addiction in your answer," said the producer quickly.

"Sure," said my dad. "It can be addicting for some kids, like drugs and alcohol. It *is* an escape. Is that what you want?"

"I think that's fine!" shouted the producer, super excited. "If you can say that, that it *can* be addictive for *some* kids. That's all we need! I'm not looking for this kid, I'm not looking for most kids—if it's possible for *one* kid out there to possibly be addicted to this, then it could be an addiction! But you can say, you're *more* concerned about the dangerous aspect."

My father looked suddenly fatigued and wary. "Right."

"So are you okay with me leaving the question then?" the producer asked gleefully. "Can this be as addictive as drugs or alcohol?"

Dad started laughing hard. "I thought you changed it!"

"But I thought you, uh, you could say that, uh, for some kids maybe . . ."

"Okay," said my father, capitulating out of sheer exhaustion.

"If you can just say *maybe*, for *some* kids, that's great."

"'Addiction' is a very strong word," said my father in his educator voice. "A more accurate word might be 'habit-forming.' It can be habitual."

"Mm-hm."

"It's a different thing."

"Mm-hm."

"So I could say, it can be habit-forming."

"Okay," said the producer, seeming annoyed for the first time. "Okay. That's perfect. Okay. So let's try it again. Okay, so I'll just say, one more time, 'Can the choking game be as addictive as drugs or alcohol?'"

"It can be a habit. A bad habit. And it can be more dangerous than drugs or alcohol. Parents have to be aware that kids do this, and they have to have a conversation with their kids, starting around eleven years of age. Don't confront them and ask them if they're doing it. Ask them if they've heard of it, and just let them talk."

—————

Just a few minutes later, finding my way to the bathroom, I passed the room where the family of the dead boy waited. The same pro-ducer was going through the show with them, just as he had with my father. He was in the midst of pretending to be Dr. Oz for a second time, reading the introduction that described the choking game and its list of monikers. As I passed the doorway, I heard him say the words "space monkey."

The show unfolded exactly as the producer foretold. Dr. G autopsied the dummy to demonstrate the difference between a suicide and a death by choking game. She showed the audience the different markings made by the rope on the neck. She took a fake enlarged brain out of the fake old man's fake head, and compared it to a fake regular brain, so we could see the differ-ence. It was gross, gross enough that I involuntarily let out a tiny shriek. The corpse was rolled offstage a bit too swiftly, like a prop in a vaudeville act. You would not, I would hope, roll a real body that fast. Dr. Oz invited the family to sit and tell their story. As soon as the family walked onto the stage, they began to cry. Dramatic images of children choking themselves were flashed in montage; my father was asked a prepared question that Dr. Oz knew my father would revise and essentially negate before answering.

After the show, the producer walked us to the exit. Down the hall, they were setting up for *Late Night with Jimmy Fallon*. The producer seemed pleased with my father's performance, and said they would be calling him again. My father left some of his self-help books with the producer, hoping he might be invited back to talk about anything other than the choking game, which had become something of a personal albatross. "We'll be calling you!" said the producer, grinning fiercely. The full force of his youthful enthusiasm washed over us in a warm, hopeful, happy light.

It was another three years before the show called on my father again, this time wanting to know if he could appear as an expert on people who eat glass.

———————

My father had expertise as someone who had worked in the field of parenting and self-help for decades. Yet he was no specialist in the choking game; the media had turned him into an authority by the very act of calling him one. By the time *The Dr. Oz Show* came around, he was well-versed in the subject; yet he was essentially fed lines by the producer, who had zero expertise or authority. Only by fighting the producer was my father able to retain some information he felt was truthful and accurate for the audience. Our acceptance of experts is predicated on a trust that behind their advice is a form of truth. If that trust is broken, we experience a disorienting loneliness, an increased burden on ourselves. We become untethered.

It reminded me of *The Wizard of Oz*, a book I'd loved as a child, but one that had also troubled me. Dorothy and her cohorts travel to see the all-powerful wizard because they believe he can grant them their utmost desires. When they finally encounter him, he turns out to be nothing but a small, impotent man behind a projector. The scene resonates with existential dread and desperation, the realization that no one is omnipotent. As a parable, it reveals the disordered nature of our lives—a fundamental underlying chaos—and the feeling of helplessness that follows that discovery. The disillusionment that Dorothy, the Cowardly Lion, the Tin Man, and the Scarecrow inevitably feel (Toto the dog, I think, is no worse off), the reckoning with their own false hope, is exactly what we all fear about self-help experts. What if there is no such thing as an expert? How will we know what to do? Can we navigate the world on our own knowledge alone? Will we be misled?

Even when you are educated enough in a subject to be considered an expert, no pat solution can resolve, or even address, the complex challenges of life. One day, as I was paging through my father's old catalogs doing research for this book, I came across a sidebar written by my father. It was about a toy he had invented called "Finger Folk." I remembered Finger Folk, mostly for the ingenious way they transmogrified: a cutout of a torso was strapped to your two fingers, which became the torso's legs. Next to a drawing of the Finger Folk my father told an anecdote featuring yours truly. When we moved to Paris, I read in his catalog, I used to "complain constantly." I didn't like all the walking (we had moved from a city where we mostly drove to one where we exclusively walked), I didn't like the strange food (I distinctly remember having to eat very salty pigs' feet in order not to insult our host one night), and I couldn't understand what anyone was saying. Tired of listening to me complain, my father invented Finger Folk. The Finger Folk had a complaint department, where I was allowed to walk my be-folked fingers over and complain about anything

I found vexing. The theory was that by creating a space for me to complain exclusively, I wouldn't complain the rest of the time. According to my father, it worked.

Reading about it almost thirty years later, I objected to my portrayal, and not only because it conflicted with my own narrative about my childhood resilience. I had been given a place to complain, but I was also forced to restrict, literally and figuratively, those complaints to the land of Finger Folk, who by reason of not being real, human folk, existed only for a certain amount of time each day. My father had solved a micro parenting problem while overlooking, or ignoring, the macro parenting problem. What he failed to see was that my problems were larger than what I was superficially complaining about. There was no complaint department big enough to contain my feelings about losing a mother, losing a country, or any of the new, perplexing, destabilizing things in my life, including but not limited to walking for long distances.

I recognized the Finger Folk not just as a game I had played, but as a sleight of hand that I had learned from my father, one where the very act of addressing an emotion represses it; where the performance of communication supplants real communication; where a structure is imposed on an emotional chaos, a structure so inherently incompatible that the emotion must retreat into the recesses of one's brain, never to return. But eventually it does return. Sometimes the only solution is to accept that there is no solution; that certain things have to be endured; that they cannot, should not, be fixed.

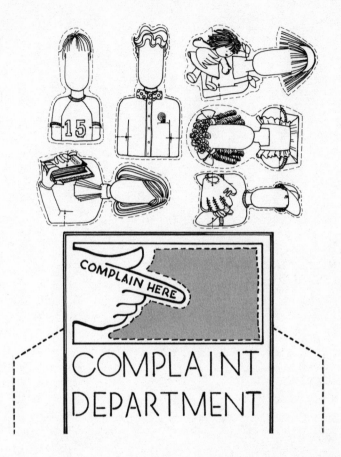

The complaint department struck me as a perfect embodiment of how my father and I had avoided talking about my mother for so long. Instead of two people confronting a problem, we interacted by means of a booth and a paper doll with finger legs. That kind of structure can provide a temporary sense of order and comfort, but it does not reflect reality.

The complaint department transformed complaints into compliance. And my own inclination to conform is why I went on to believe for years that my mother had died in a car accident, even though that was not the truth.

5

THE SECRET IS
NOT a SECRET

Vision Boards and the Law of Attraction

In March 2007, my father and I sat behind three collapsible plastic exhibit tables piled with products from his catalog. A well-known lecturer on autism was giving a two-day workshop, and our plan was to sell my father's products to the attendees. Items for sale that day included a time-out mat; Constructive Eating silverware (looks like construction machinery); Tangle Therapy (a plastic twisty purple thing you wring into different shapes, because repetitive movement is thought to release serotonin); and around a dozen Dr. Playwell's games (Dr. Playwell is a cartoon version of my dad) with names like the Think Positive Game and the Fantastical Feelings Machine. We also offered something called Counseling Balls (which we sold a ton of, though I still couldn't explain to you how they work) and Positive Attitude Balls (you catch the ball and your left thumb lands on an imperative like "Say what makes you happy," or "Do a silly dance," or "Make an animal noise"). My dad said, "It's so simple.

That's why people like it. And it's queer." My dad threw me the ball, delighted. I refused to make an animal noise.

Without the financial resources of a self-help guru like MVH or Dr. Phil, my father still had several other jobs. One of them included traveling to places where parents and therapists congregate, setting up his booth, and trying to sell products. Our first sale was at 8 a.m. A woman bought a Tangle Therapy and an Ungame, and while my father small-talked her, counselors, parents, and social workers—overwhelmingly women, overwhelmingly white— swarmed the table, knocking things over as if they had bear paws for hands. People asked me questions, assuming I was knowledgeable about the products—*What are the best products for five-year-olds? Do you have more copies of The Ungame?*—and I tried to stall them while my dad helped other customers.

When someone asked me the price of something, I diligently looked it up; when they asked my father, he quoted the first number that popped into his head. As a result we sold Tangle Therapy for twenty dollars, twelve dollars, and eight dollars, all in a span of five minutes. I started to worry that someone would notice and the lot of them would revolt. The record-keeping was also problematic; my dad's modus operandi was to handwrite a receipt, which he would then throw on the floor, along with any cash or change people brought us. I found an empty cardboard box for him to throw the receipts and the cash in, but he would not be persuaded.

"The floor's fine," he shrugged. "We'll pick it up later."

Organization has never been my father's strong suit. He likes to tell people about his filing system, which consists of three drawers. Incoming documents go in the first drawer. After a month, he moves the contents of the first drawer to the second drawer. After another month, he moves the contents of the second drawer to the third drawer. After another month, he throws the contents of the third drawer away. My father feels his filing method is sufficient, arguing that if he doesn't need something for three months, he probably doesn't need it at all. As someone who owns a label maker, I find that this system makes my skin blister.

A tall, busty blonde wearing a tight T-shirt from the Center for Autism Research wandered over from another table, which was covered in small polyester brains. I had picked one up earlier; they were pleasantly squishy.

"Wow," she said.

"Most of this stuff isn't readily available," said my father.

"There might be a reason for that," I muttered under my breath.

"I have a child on the spectrum myself," she said to my father, ignoring me.

I asked her what the Center for Autism Research did. She responded, unhelpfully, that they do research on autism.

"What kind of research?"

"All kinds. Some animal research."

My heart sank. I was afraid to ask, but I did anyway. "What sort of animal research?"

"They've isolated all the genes in a mouse," she explained.

"Even sarcasm!" my dad piped in.

"They can manipulate them and essentially make an autistic mouse," she said.

"Wow," I said, frowning, trying to picture an autistic mouse, thinking gloomily about a very affecting book from my childhood, *Flowers for Algernon.*

The CAR lady asked if we had anything for "older kids, and, like, feelings?" Dad recommended The Ungame. He also gave her a five-dollar discount on Tangle Therapy and a free feelings poster. He called it an "exhibitor discount," but I suspected it might be a hot-lady discount.

As my father and I waited for the next wave, the TV in the lobby announced dramatically, "Fertility! If you're over thirty, you should get on with it." I was thirty-one, and not only was I not getting on with it, I was in a hotel lobby selling The Ungame with my father. Against my better judgment I turned my head to watch; a professional-looking woman in a white skirt suit explained in a sympathetic and conspiratorial voice that if you're over thirty-five you "get babies with, you know, reproductive things and, you know, problems."

When anyone walked in or out of the conference room, likely on a trip to the bathroom, we asked them without fail, "Would you like a free feelings poster? Feelings? Animal Feelings?" That was my cue to roll up a poster and secure it with a rubber band, while my father said something gratuitous and superfluous like "We love feelings!" We also offered to send them a digital copy if they would kindly give us their e-mail address. My dad said he was sometimes shocked by the e-mail addresses counselors used.

"Some people write, 'screwyou@amazon.com,' or 'crazy pirate,' 'hotnready'—it's shocking what professionals use as their e-mails. It's shocking."

"That's gross."

My dad righted a fallen Awesome Awards box, where one makes one's own prize ribbons for doing awesome things like washing the dishes.

"This would be good for your next party," he said, holding the box up. I promised to keep it in mind.

By lunchtime, I was exhausted. People wandered by every

so often and accidentally knocked down the display. "How many times has that happened?" asked the latest perpetrator. "A lot," I said, not bothering to hide my annoyance.

Since I refused to play with him, my dad played with the You & Me Ball by himself. It landed on "Say something you're sorry about."

He paused for thoughtful consideration. "I'm not sorry about anything." He threw the ball in the air again. It landed on "What is one rule you always follow?" He thought about this, staring off into the distance.

"I'm always polite."

I knew we were officially bored when my father began practicing a dance he called "Going Nowhere." The dance involved walking as though on a treadmill, shuffling your feet so that you go nowhere. He took my smile as encouragement, and worked on another version of the dance, "Going Nowhere Fast." (Same dance, faster.) My father has been performing this dance for me as far back as I can remember, usually in public. Though it used to embarrass me, I now barely notice the dance, which is why my father has to shout "Going Nowhere!" just to get my attention as he shuffles his feet forward and back.

At the end of the day, I helped my father pack his products into their boxes, and we loaded them back into the car. It seemed like we had about as much stuff as we had come with. He had paid three hundred dollars for a table and an exhibit in the hallway, and hoped to make a thousand dollars selling products and get one hundred names for his mailing list (he calculated that each name was worth $1.50, based on what he would otherwise have to pay for an ad on Google). We had made only seven hundred dollars. This didn't seem like a favorable outcome, considering my father had also paid for hotel rooms and gas. Yet he was characteristically optimistic about the experience.

"It's almost enough to cover our costs. Plus we got fifty names for the mailing list. That's good. And we had fun, right?"

I smiled, but didn't answer him.

He insisted, "Right?"

"Right."

My father's concept of success derives from the "how you play the game" school. He values process over product; any enterprise in which he has fun carries some intrinsic value. For those who are more result oriented, there is no shortage of self-help books on success. One of the most popular schemes for prosperity is called the law of attraction. This law, backed by no widely accepted evidence, posits that you can attract things you want simply by thinking about them.

Although the law of attraction could theoretically be applied to anything, it most frequently appears in self-help books about making money. In *Practical Methods for Self-Development* (1904), Elizabeth Towne claimed that money was as free as air. She wrote, "The only thing that keeps us from taking plenty of money or air is fear. . . . The trouble with us is that we are afraid to expand. . . . Take deep, full breaths of air, and your mind and purse expand in sympathy with your lungs. . . . Money is really as free as air."

The rich "do not get rich because they possess talents and abilities that other men have not, but because they happened to do things in a Certain Way," wrote Wallace D. Wattles, author of the best-selling tome *The Science of Getting Rich*. A thin man, with a long, wan face, Wallace D. Wattles was an admirer of Horace Fletcher, the author of *Menticulture,* a self-help book on the virtues of prolonged mastication, and Edward H. Dewey, Fletcher's mentor and creator of the "No-Breakfast Diet." In 1908, Wattles ran for office as a member of the Socialist party. Wattles died in 1911, just one year after the publication of *The Science of Getting Rich.* The book was not only an instant best seller, it is still published and revered today. This fact is even more impressive when one reads the book and realizes how far from the line demarcating sanity Wattles has wandered.

Wattles claims the science of getting rich is as "exacting and logical" as algebra and arithmetic. However, he instructs you to do things only "in a Certain Way." It's a long time before he explains to you what this Certain Way is, and then only by defining it with a bunch of other amorphous terms like having "Faith" and believing in the idea that you are an "Advancing Man."*

The following passage is emblematic of his blunt but effective style:

> Talented people get rich, and blockheads get rich; intellectually brilliant people get rich, and very stupid people get rich; physically strong people get rich, and weak and sickly people get rich . . . any man or woman who has sense enough to read and understand these words can certainly get rich.

Wattles's use of repetition is almost unparalleled in a genre largely based on repetition. Repetition is a favorite rhetorical tool in self-help. Repetition is how we learn. It's an old adage in advertising

---

*I came to love the phrase "Certain Way," as well as "Advancing Man" (so promising, so threatening: both men and armies advance).

that you need to see something seven times before it takes residence in your brain. Repetition is also thought to promote understanding, create familiarity, imprint memory, generate Pavlovian cues, and sometimes send people into a trancelike state. In this instance, the repetition of "get rich" is bound to be pleasing to someone who is interested in getting rich.

You should not allow the lack of "visible" opportunity to dissuade you from believing in invisible possibilities, argued Wattles. This, I warn you, is where it gets weird.

> *Everything you see on earth is made from one original substance, out of which all things proceed* [his emphasis]. New Forms are constantly being made, and older ones are dissolving; but all are shapes assumed by One Thing. There is no limit to the supply of Formless Stuff, or Original Substance.

"Formless Stuff" does not clarify things for me, explanationwise. "Stuff" is vague, and when modified by "formless" it connotes even less. We should not be surprised, then, when Formless Stuff acts in confusing and hard-to-understand ways. I have to admit I never comprehended Formless Stuff. When my eyes weren't glazing over, my time reading this book was mostly occupied by writing "crazy!" and "so crazy!" in the margins. If you need further convincing, imagine you are at a cocktail party and someone says this to you: "The universe of forms has been made by Formless Living Substance, throwing itself into form in order to express itself more fully." Might you confiscate that person's car keys?

"What the mind of man can conceive and believe, it can achieve," wrote Napoleon Hill, author of 1937's *Think and Grow Rich*, now one of the best-selling self-help books of all time (30 million copies). Born in 1883, Hill was a handsome man who started his career as a journalist. His life changed when he was sent on an assignment to interview Andrew Carnegie about the secrets of his success. Carnegie was impressed with Hill, and commissioned him to interview five hundred of America's most affluent men. The twenty-year project eventually provided the basis for *Think and Grow Rich*. Hill later became an advisor to both Woodrow Wilson and FDR.

Hill writes, "In every chapter of this book, mention has been made of the money-making secret which has made fortunes for more than five hundred exceedingly wealthy men whom I have carefully analyzed over a long period of years." Said secret was cryptically confided to Hill by none other than his sponsor Andrew Carnegie, that "canny loveable old Scotsman," who afterward sat back in his chair "with a merry twinkle in his eyes." Hill says,

> The secret to which I refer has been mentioned no fewer than a hundred times, throughout this book. It has not been directly named, for it seems to work more successfully when it is merely uncovered and left in sight, where THOSE WHO ARE READY, and SEARCHING FOR IT, may pick it up. That is why Mr. Carnegie tossed it to me so quietly, without giving me its specific name.

Because the secret is not directly named, the reader is left with only a vague impression. Explications of the law of attraction were consistently so abstract they verged on incoherence. I often wondered if the language was intentionally obscure; a message not "directly named" cannot be easily discredited. I found this irritating, yet I was more than compensated by an entertaining section where Hill describes practicing "character-building" through autosuggestion.

He holds "imaginary Council meetings" in which he speaks aloud to his imaginary Cabinet members (Napoleon, Lincoln, Emerson, among others) and asks for their advice. Not content to merely speak to his conjured and dead mentors, Hill creates an entire world where his heroes come to life. As you read, please keep in mind that this person was an advisor to two American presidents:

> After some months of this nightly procedure, I was astounded by the discovery that these imaginary figures became, apparently, real.
>
> Each of these nine men developed individual characteristics, which surprised me. For example, Lincoln developed the habit of always being late, then walking around in solemn parade. When he came, he walked very slowly, with his hands clasped behind him, and once in a while, he would stop as he passed, and rest his hand, momentarily, upon my shoulder. . . .
>
> Burbank and Paine often indulged in witty repartee which seemed, at times, to shock the other members of the cabinet. . . .
>
> On one occasion Burbank was late. When he came he was excited with enthusiasm, and explained that he had been late, because of an experiment he was making, through which he hoped to be able to grow apples on any sort of tree. Paine chided him by reminding him that it was an apple which started all the trouble between man and woman. Darwin chuckled heartily as he suggested that Paine should watch out for little serpents, when he went into the forest to gather apples, as they had the habit of growing into big snakes. Emerson observed—"No serpents, no apples," and Napoleon [Bonaparte] remarked, "No apples, no state!"

In 1960, an insurance magnate named W. Clement Stone published a book with Napoleon Hill called *Success Through a Positive Mental*

Attitude (PMA). Like so many self-help authors, Stone rose from hardship and poverty to wealth and success. His father died when Stone was three, leaving the family with gambling debts. Stone worked selling newspapers, and at sixteen began working for his mother's insurance agency in Detroit. He expanded that first insurance agency under the name Combined Insurance Company of America; by 1930, he had a thousand insurance agents working for him. The author of *The Success System That Never Fails* (1962), *The Other Side of the Mind* (1964, with Norma Lee Browning), and the aforementioned *Success Through a Positive Mental Attitude,* Stone also founded a monthly magazine called *Success Unlimited,* and had a series of lectures with Napoleon Hill, which they called PMA: Science of Success. Stone contributed millions of dollars to Nixon's campaigns. The size of his contributions eventually led to congressional discussion of campaign spending limits. He lived to be one hundred years old.

A short man with a thin mustache, Stone began each day by shouting, "I feel happy! I feel healthy! I feel terrific!" He was an exuberant dresser, and if he felt people were not paying sufficient attention to him, he would randomly shout, "Bingo!" (This detail reminded me of my father.)

Stone's slogans, and presentation of ideas, were strikingly laconic. For instance, he urged his employees to psych themselves up to sell insurance by simply shouting, "Do It Now!" Stone ran his insurance company, which still operates today, using his PMA philosophy.

Stone reiterated what is essentially the politically conservative heart of self-help. He urged the reader to stop blaming society and to take personal responsibility for their failures; the onus is on the individual, not the government or any other institution. Stone writes,

These people are all saying, in essence, that the world has given them a raw deal. . . . They start out with a negative mental attitude. And, of course, with that attitude, they *are* handicapped. But it is NMA [Negative Mental Attitude] that is holding them down, not the external handicap which they give as the cause of their failure.

After I read Wattles and Hill, Stone's theories began to sound reasonable to me, if only because I understood them and because no dead people came back to life.

I'd first encountered a vision board when I interviewed Vanessa Ferreira just after the 2008 financial crisis. A former finance person (this is as specific a job description as you'll ever get from me for someone who works in finance) who found herself unemployed, Ferreira had started a website called the Millionaire Mind Experiment. The purpose of the website was, evidently, to make a million dollars just by thinking about it.

Ferreira had written on the site, "Most of us are familiar with movies like *The Secret, What the Bleep Do We Know,* and Wayne Dyer's *The Shift,* but how many of us have attempted to use the Law of Attraction but soon enough lost focus and gave up?" I was not, in fact, familiar with any of those things, but I was intrigued. She reassured readers that participating would not be time-consuming or challenging, saying, "All you have to do is gently hold the following affirmation in your mind one to three times a day: I intend to attract One Million Dollars into my life and into the lives of everyone who holds this intention." She believed that the more people she could convince to participate, the more power the group would have to attract money. She was not dogmatic or overpromising, she just asked that you "keep an open mind, and just allow the law of attraction to work its magic."

Ferreira was a pretty woman in her thirties whose decorating indicated a penchant for beige tones. When I visited her apartment in New Jersey she gave me a glass of water and showed me her vision board. It was nothing fancy: a white, three-paneled poster board, the exact same kind I used at my fourth grade science fair when I proved, once and for all, that jelly molds faster than peanut butter. Each panel was covered in pictures, mostly magazine cutouts. There was a picture of her looking svelte in a bikini. "This is a picture of me when I was thin," she explained, saying that she hoped to lose some weight. She pointed to some pictures of fit people doing yoga in yoga clothes. There were pictures of exotic-looking beaches, and generic blissful-looking couples walking on those beaches, feeling, one presumes, generic blissful feelings. There were pictures of some nice real estate properties. "I want a house," Ferreira said.

Ferreira explained to me how the vision board worked. You collect images—from magazines, photographs, etc.—that depict your desires. They can be abstract, like a picture you believe represents love, or concrete, like a photo of a yacht. She had made this board with her fiancé. "This is my side, this is his side," she said. "He didn't believe too much in it, but I introduced him to a lot of these things, and he's really enjoying it. We wanted a new TV, and we got it in no time."

The Millionaire Mind Experiment, she explained, was based on the concept of manifesting. The word "manifest" is related to "manifesto," a public declaration of aims, and is derived from *manifestare* (to make public) and *manifestus* (obvious). I remembered being fond of the concept of Manifest Destiny in high school, mostly because I liked the word combination. None of those definitions precisely describe how Ferreira understood manifesting.

"For example," she said, "my fiancé and I wanted to move to Florida. A month and a half ago, we told ourselves, 'Let's make it happen, let's manifest it.' You put out the intention—'This is what I want for myself'—and then you manifest it. We really feel like within three weeks, we had manifested it. We had attracted it. There was no doubt in our minds that it was going to happen. But it wasn't that it just happened, or it wasn't because of our actions. Yeah, our actions made a difference, but it was the *intention* that we put out there to the universe. My belief, and the beliefs of people who follow the law of attraction, is that our thoughts create our reality."

Our thoughts *do* create our reality: they are the sole mechanism through which our experience of the world is filtered. The notion that it's easier to accomplish things when we believe that we can is common sense and widely understood. The other day on the subway I overheard two nine-year-olds conversing. One nine-year-old said to the other, "But it's never going to happen." The other nine-year-old retorted, condescendingly, "Not with *that* attitude."

But people who believe in the law of attraction interpret the relationship between thoughts and action more literally. They believe one's internal reality impacts not just the way one subjectively experiences an external reality, but the objective external reality itself. In the world of psychology, believing that your mind can control reality is called "magical thinking."

In 2007, the law of attraction was repackaged, yet again, in a DVD called *The Secret*, and soon after in a book of the same name. The book was a considerable hit, selling 19 million copies worldwide. Author Rhonda Byrne was a guest on *The Oprah Winfrey Show*, the sine qua non of self-help advice in America. Byrne claimed that "you can have whatever you want in life." Byrne writes that her daughter handed her a 100-year-old book (though unnamed, I'm pretty sure it's *The Science of Getting Rich*), containing "the Secret." Byrne begins the book with the inspirational story template: Her life had "collapsed"; her father had died; her relationships were "in turmoil." "Little did I know at the time," she writes, "out of my despair was to come the greatest gift."

Yes, readers, Byrne discovered "the Secret," a knowledge so transforming that she had to research it: "I couldn't believe all the people who knew this. They were the greatest people in history: Plato, Shakespeare, Newton, Hugo, Beethoven, Lincoln, Emerson, Edison, Einstein. Incredulous, I asked, 'Why doesn't *everyone* know this?'"

Incredulous, I answered: Lady, everyone *does* know this. Both *The Secret* and books like *Think and Grow Rich* would have you believe that the law of attraction had purposely been hidden (the movie *The Secret* shows people wearing chain mail and other various period costumes burying and burning unspecified texts, which we can only assume have something to do with the Secret) because, I guess, if it's hidden it must be worth uncovering. But the concepts in *The Secret* have been published in books that anyone can buy—and have bought, in the millions—for at least a hundred years. Furthermore, something you don't know is not necessarily a secret; it's just something you don't know. For instance, I don't know anything about rocket science, but that doesn't make rocket science a *secret*.

Despite being endlessly referenced, the Secret isn't explained. One quoted expert compares it to electricity, saying that the fact that he doesn't understand how electricity works doesn't preclude him from believing in electricity. The book does, however, offer concrete suggestions on how to turn your negative thoughts into positive ones.

Here's a freebie: If you're sad, think of babies.

For the most part, belief in the law of attraction, while questionable, is benign; while the concept may not result in anything concrete, it probably won't harm you either. There are, however, exceptions. In *The Secret*, Bill Harris, a teacher and founder of the Centerpointe Research Institute, tells an inspirational story about Robert, a gay student. According to Harris, Robert's homosexuality made his life "grim." Robert's coworkers were abusive to him. Random people on the street "accosted" him (Harris doesn't specify whether verbally or physically). When he performed his stand-up comedy, says Harris, "everybody heckled him about being gay. His whole life was one of unhappiness and misery." Harris told Robert that he was focusing on the negative—i.e., abusive attacks on his sexuality—and not on the positive. The problem wasn't bigotry; it was Robert. According to Harris:

> Then [Robert] started taking this thing about focusing on what you want to heart, and he began really trying it. What happened within the next six to eight weeks was an absolute miracle. All the people in his office who had been harassing him either transferred to another department, quit working at the company, or started completely leaving him alone. He began to love his job. When he walked down the street, nobody harassed him anymore. They just weren't there. When he did his stand-up comedy routines he started getting standing ovations, and nobody was heckling him!

This story fills me with dread for the human condition. A recurring criticism of self-help is that by assigning all responsibility to the individual it unfairly absolves the society from culpability. This story not only illustrates that flaw perfectly, it exposes why it's a morally untenable position. Instead of a call to arms for education or law enforcement or governmental protections, the burden of change is entirely on Robert. The law of attraction is unidirectional; it doesn't fail you, you fail it.

Byrne writes,

> Often when people first hear this part of the Secret they recall events in history where masses of lives were lost, and they find it incomprehensible that so many people could have attracted themselves to the event. By the law of attraction, they had to be on the same frequency as the event. It doesn't necessarily mean they thought of that exact event, but the frequency of their thoughts matched the frequency of the event. If people believe they can be in the wrong place at the wrong time, and they have no control over outside circumstances, those thoughts of fear, separation, and powerlessness, if persistent, can attract them to being in the wrong place at the wrong time.

The average reader of *The Secret* is assumed to have only a passing familiarity with the concept of "frequency." Anyone who has ever used a radio has a vague understanding that this mechanism allows them to tune into a specific frequency, chosen from an infinite number of frequencies. In her metaphor, Byrnes is arguing that thoughts act as tuners, which "tune" people into the frequency of disaster, thereby "transmitting" disaster into their lives.

But the metaphor starts to fall apart if you follow it through. What sorts of thoughts put one on the same frequency as a genocide? What are genocide-y thoughts? What are rape-y and murder-y thoughts? And how many people who are raped and murdered really go around thinking rapey and murdery thoughts? Immensely horrifying things happen in the world, and why they happen has long been debated by religious leaders, philosophers, cultural theorists, and all sorts of brilliant thinkers who have been unable to summarily account for the pronounced unfairness, and sometimes tragic nature, of life. Attributing it all to "frequencies" seems insipid and uncharitable and dim-witted.

Note that the author refers to "events in history" instead of naming specific events. No one so far in the book has hesitated to proffer specific rewards to those who practice the law of attraction: yachts, jobs, life partners, cars, and even parking spaces. So why the sudden generality? Once you swap, say, "the 1994 Rwandan genocide" for "events in history," Byrne's already unpalatable argument gets even harder to swallow.

You may remember from high school a logical fallacy called *post hoc, ergo propter hoc,* which translates to "after this, therefore on account of it." One is tempted to assume that two successive events are connected when in fact they may have no relationship whatsoever. Or their relationship is not the one you assumed. If I were to shove you, and you were to subsequently fall down, we could presume that my shove was the cause of your fall. However, it would also be possible to argue that you tripped over a stick while trying to avoid the shove, that you had a seizure, or that you fell intentionally to flatter my sense of strength. In Byrne's worldview, you fell because you believed you would fall.

Self-fulfilling prophecies, placebo effects: we don't know exactly how they work, but they do. Cause-and-effect relationships are difficult to isolate, and books like *The Secret* take advantage of this. We are pattern-seeking creatures, and we want the world to make sense. We readily accept mistruths so that the stories we tell ourselves can add up. Byrne offers her readers an undeniably seductive amount of control over the narrative of their lives, one that is difficult for many, if not all of us, to resist.

———

The concrete and inexpensive parameters of the vision board made it the perfect conduit to experiment with the law of attraction. I enlisted a college friend, Cynthia, to be my test subject. She was skeptical, but ready to try anything; she had been in a period of sustained frustration both at her job and in her personal life. We agreed that we would make her a board together, and she would allow me to report on what happened over a three-month period.

I went to the nearest art store and bought a giant piece of Styrofoam board ($4.43). When the store employee asked me what kind of project I was doing I pretended not to hear her. I also assembled scissors, tape, and glue, and told Cynthia to bring some magazines we could pillage for images.

The day we met happened to be April Fool's Day, which was not the most auspicious start. I dimmed the lights and lit some candles, a necessary prop, I guessed, for all liminal crafts (séances, spell-casting, vision-board–making). Cynthia brought wine, and a selection of magazines: *Outside, Vanity Fair, The Economist, National Geographic Traveler, Surface, Paper, Went,* and the *Atlantic Monthly.* I poured two generous glasses of wine and we began our search.

As she paged through the magazines, Cynthia was initially apprehensive. "What bothers me is, these aren't things for which you're striving or working. It's not exactly cheating, but . . . it lacks common sense." Then she reflected on what she had said. "But you know what? Maybe I just think everything has to be climbed like an impossible ice wall."

She dutifully put her reservations aside and dedicated herself to the task at hand. She ripped a page out of a magazine and held it up. "Okay, this is awesome." The page read, "Traversing Mordor," and showed an image of a barren, forbidding, icy, craggy place. It was the last place I would ever choose to vacation. "I would do this in a second." She ripped out another page. "See this sad backpacker, sitting on a rock? I want that."

In the way that divergent aspects of close friends' personalities can become polarized, Cynthia and I often acted out a mutually agreed-upon narrative in which she was a risk-taker and I was risk-averse; where she made everything more difficult than it had to be and I made everything too easy; where she preferred to climb a mountain and I preferred to lie in a hammock. Basically, in our lesser moments where we tended to oversimplify, I characterized her as a masochist and she characterized me as a sloth.

She flipped through the magazines methodically. A pleasant rhythm developed: *thwap, thwap, thwap.* Occasionally she paused to say, "Hmmm . . ." or "Hamburg, Germany?" *Paper* magazine was a disappointment. "No dreams in *Paper.* Just judgment," she said, tossing the magazine over her shoulder.

She flipped faster through the pages, singing, "I don't want a cat, I don't want a beach umbrella, I don't want a car, I don't want to dance with a white horse."

"Is it fun to think about what you want?" I interrupted.

"You have to have a certain amount of confidence or delusion. But this is fun! It's like shopping. There's a weird pressure to remember everything you want or you won't get it."

Cutting out a diamond-encrusted Chanel watch, she said,

"This just represents having more time. I want more time to write. Diamond-strong time." A minute later: "I want a dog, why not?" She put a dog on the board. "That would be a bummer if that were the only thing that came to pass." Minutes later, the dog was cut. "He's too crazy-staring-looking." She wasn't exactly talking to me. I sometimes felt as if I could have walked away without her noticing, so engrossed was she in shopping for her future.

Certain themes began to emerge. Cynthia wanted more time to pursue creative projects, a job where she felt respected, a relationship, a life with travel and exploration, and a bicycle. She had always been a fearless traveler and known for jumping into bodies of cold water when no one else would even consider it. In the past few years she had been fixated on riding solo across America on a bicycle. This plan held no appeal for me whatsoever, and I was constantly trying to talk her out of it.

"Is that safe?" I would ask. "What will you eat? How will you go to the bathroom? Where will you sleep?"

For Cynthia, the only real obstacle was that she didn't have a bicycle. Accordingly, there were many pictures of bikes on the board. She frowned at the pictures. "It's a little cyclist heavy," she admitted.

"How many bikes do you have on there?"

"At least six. Out of twenty or so images." She grudgingly cut one.

Once the magazines had all been parsed and mined, it was time to glue. Cynthia stood over the board like a war general, moving images here and there with confidence and intensity. She took off her jacket and rolled up her sleeves, making thoughtful clicking noises with her tongue. She stopped speaking to me entirely, working diligently and silently. A few minutes later she suddenly asked me, "Do you have a picture of Samuel Beckett?" I Googled him, found an image, and printed out his face. I was cutting his face out of a sheet of paper when I became hesitant.

"Wait, why are we putting Beckett on the board?" I was cutting out his head from a biography that talked about his loneliness, depression, and drinking. According to this source he'd once said, "I had little talent for happiness," and had remarked after a failed romantic encounter that he was dead and had no feelings that were human.

"I like that quote of his about 'fail again, fail better,'" she said.

Against my better judgment, I handed over Beckett's head.

"This is an image of health and strength and independence," she said, looking at a picture of a lone hiker. She frowned. "One starts using the language so quickly.

"So far the vision board is working amazingly," she announced. "It makes me feel good and light and happy."

"Why do you think you're feeling happy?"

"It converts abstract problems in a game. You disconnect from the actual problem and start paying attention to the rules of the game. When you solve the game, you feel like you've solved the abstract problem."

"Do you feel empowered?" I asked.

"I do. I feel weirdly clearheaded, as though I'm solving an actual problem."

"When are you going to start gluing the images to the board?"

"I need a drink first."

She poured herself another glass of wine and stepped back to survey the board. "All of these images please me," she announced with finality and satisfaction.

Within a few minutes, however, she had changed her mind. "Hm. I'm a little stressed all of the sudden. I'm not sure how these last things fit. For a second I was like, I know exactly what I want. Now I don't know."

My patience waned. The wine had made me sleepy, and this was taking longer than I'd anticipated. "Just glue something," I pressed.

She slid some images to one side of the board. "These are things I'm on the fence about."

"Why are you being so finicky?"

"I believe if I were to do this wrong—and this surprises me that I feel this way—I could bring some misery or trouble into my life."

It went on like this for a while. Here is a sampling of my notes.

9:18 P.M.

Me: Have you glued anything down yet?

C: I'm close. I have commitment issues.

9:37 P.M.

Upon applying the first bit of glue: "Here goes. This is no fucking joke. I'm really doing this. I'm stressed. I feel nervous and excited. I wish I were saying this for effect. But this feels real."

9:43 P.M.

More moving of images. Still only one has been glued down.

9:50 P.M.

Budget gets glued! Wait. It's ripped off. Not straight enough. Back down. She has been silent for a few minutes, but speaks as though she were in the middle of saying something: "Also, in order to take a trip like this I have to be able to pay for it, so . . ." "Mm-hm," I say.

10:01 P.M.

> Announces, "I need a green element." Back to magazines. Cuts out a leaf, cutting carefully around every jagged edge. So sleepy.

10:03 P.M.

> Beckett gets glued.

10:05 P.M.

> Me: What's your state of mind right now?
>
> C: Calm and happy. I keep thinking I could have laid this out better, but things don't have to be perfect to move forward.
>
> Me: You've become very philosophical in the last hour.
>
> C: Revelations are sticking to me like glue!*

By 10:30 the last image had been glued down. I was now prone on the couch. "Done!" she announced. Looking at her vision board felt curiously intimate, like I was peering inside her brain. We wrapped the board in a black garbage bag so she could take it home on the subway without exposing her hopes and dreams to strangers.

The next morning she e-mailed me. Despite having an ant infestation and waking up late for work, she said when she looked at the vision board she felt better.

> I really did. I think because the optimistic/excited about the future part of my brain is essentially captured in vision-board amber there, and I recognized it right away. (Does this mean my mind is starting to become magnetized? I think it might.)

---

*The word "revelations," which she had cut from a magazine, was stuck to her arm.

Two days after we made the vision board, I read a profile of a songwriter named Ester Dean. Dean attributed her success to a vision board; she claimed that she'd watched the movie version of *The Secret* in 2008, made a vision board, and by 2012 had achieved everything on the board. That same day, Cynthia told me she'd received a tax refund from the IRS. She wrote,

> I had, to my great surprise, come home last night to find a tax
> refund from the IRS, a surprise check worth $467. The money
> suddenly felt like VB money, money attracted rather than
> earned—ridiculous but compelling—and I scanned the mental
> board again, hoping to match the sum with the ticket price of
> one of my material desires.

Months earlier, she had owed the IRS $900; now they owed her enough money that not only was her debt covered, she was getting checks from them. This was conceivably due to the fact that she had stopped doing her own taxes and had sprung for an accountant, but the timing made it seem possible that the board had worked its magic. *Post hoc, ergo propter hoc.* When two of her friends heard about it, they wanted to make vision boards. Cynthia then replicated the scene from my apartment with her two friends, while continuing to add to her own board.

This was an unexpected turn of events. The initially apprehensive Cynthia had turned proselytizer. I could accede to the pull of the law of attraction, but I found it difficult to understand. Was it a subgenre of the power of positive thinking, one focused with needlelike precision on objects and scenarios? It seemed more fun to be actively engaged in a specific fantasy than to merely have a positive attitude. But even more than with positive thinking, I worried that the vision board was encouraging my friends to enter into uncharted territories of delusion. I wanted the vision board to act as a model, but not a template. As someone who likes it when my friends are happy, I appreciated the emotional triage the vision board seemed to perform. There was something of value in it. But value is different from "it works." And there was something bothersome in how tidy it was; all of one's hopes and dreams laid out like a map on a cheap piece of poster board. The slogan of the New York Lottery is "Hey, you never know."* The slogan appeals to the minuscule kernel of truth that makes this particular world turn, and how small a fingerhold we need to cling to the near-impossible.

Then again, I don't think fantasy is inherently destructive, and not every exercise has to produce results. Every few years I'll see a woman on the street who looks how I imagine my mother might look now, had she lived, and I'll indulge in a fantasy in which she didn't really die, but faked her own death, possibly because she was in the CIA or for another very good reason, and that she has been alive all this time and is in fact just across 86th Street, shopping for groceries like any normal, living person. I don't think this is a particularly harmful fantasy because only part of my mind believes it, and I enjoy believing in an alternate reality for a few seconds. I don't know why, but it makes me feel happy. I never approach the woman, but I imagine how overjoyed she would be to see me, how all would be forgiven.

---

*A sampling of some other lottery slogans, past and present, by state: "Someone's gotta win" (MA); "Imagine what a buck could do!" (CA); "What kind of mega millionaire would you be?" (MN); "It's gravy, baby!" (OR); "Give your dreams a chance" (NJ); "Dream big. Win big" (AZ); "Somebody's going to win, might as well be you!" (KY); and the refreshingly realistic "Benefits Older Pennsylvanians. Every Day" (PA).

For a grown woman whose mother has been dead more than thirty years, this is the most preposterous scenario I can imagine. I am more likely to win the lottery than I am to raise the dead. But still, when I see that woman, there is enough ephemeral truth for my brain to cling to, enough, for a few moments, to create an entirely alternate reality, one that I can enter, feel feelings in, have entire conversations with my undead age-appropriate mother in, and then leave behind in a way that is not devastating but surprisingly gentle. I am delivered back into the real world with a tenderness that, I choose to believe, is mother-like.

6

A FELLOWSHIP OF NERVOUS FREAKS

Overcoming Phobias and Fears

I am afraid of crowds, elevators, and heights. I am—to such a degree that I avoid it entirely—afraid of flying. People in my life, even people who know me well, are always surprised to hear I am afraid of flying, because my not flying is something few people have occasion to witness. Not flying is less obvious than not leaving the house (agoraphobia) or not going to parties (social phobia). Not flying is generally an inconspicuous event; although at age twenty-one I dropped a boyfriend off at the end of the highway exit ramp to the airport because I was too afraid even to drive up to the terminal. As if, while I waited thirty seconds for him to unload his bags, a plane might crash into my car. But fear is not reasonable. Fear dwells in the realm of imagination, where anything is possible; except, of course, one's perfect safety. In the world of fear, walking down the street and *not* having a piano fall on your head is the least likely scenario.

I think part of me believed that my fear was charming, because it resulted in ridiculous stories, such as the one about the time I took a four-day train ride to Seattle rather than fly. I was the only non-octogenarian on that excruciatingly long voyage, during which I lived entirely on PowerBars and tiny bottles of wine. The train attendants had taken to calling me "New York," and every time I walked into the dining car they would shout, "Here comes New York!" Consequently, I left my tiny berth only once a day, when I walked the length of the train to buy four single-serving bottles of red wine that I shoved furtively into my purse, once prompting the train café proprietor to remark, "You're my kind of lady!"

My fear was not charming to people who wanted to travel with me, but that was an extremely small percentage of people. My father was one of those unfortunates. My father traveled frequently, usually by himself. Despite the fact that I always said no, he continually invited me to exciting destinations that required a plane trip. (That trip we took to Atlanta to see MVH? I drove, by myself, from New York.) In 1999, he had talked me into attending a fear-of-flying self-help group. The facilitator was a former fearful flyer herself. We met every Thursday night at LaGuardia Airport. The first day the instructor asked each of us what, specifically, we were afraid of. "I'm afraid of the wings falling off the plane," said one woman. All the other people in the room afraid of the wings falling off—let's call them the Wings People—nodded, and said, "Yes," and "Amen," and showed nonverbal forms of agreement like smacking a triumphant hand on the table, vigorous head-bobbing, grave furrowing of eyebrows. Meanwhile, everyone else, myself included, thought this was the most ludicrous thing we had ever heard. The *wings* falling off? We rolled our eyes at each other. We smirked.

Then someone said, "I'm afraid of turbulence." I was one of

the Turbulence People. We Turbulence People were stone-faced, nodding in pensive, moribund agreement that turbulence was the greatest threat to mankind since smallpox, measles, etc. The Wings People looked bemused and rolled *their* eyes and shook *their* heads at what they perceived to be an entirely unwarranted fear. It went on this way for a while, the room factioning into the Explode in Midair People, the Surprise Lightning Storm People, the Plane Might Just Fall Out of the Skys, the What If We Run Out of Oxygens. Each of us had our own hierarchy of fear, where My Personal Fear was at the top of the list and Other People's Fear was unfathomable. An unlucky few started to fear new things they hadn't previously considered. The whole scene was dismaying. If we couldn't even be sympathetic to each other's fears, how could we expect anyone unafraid of flying to relate to us? More concerning still: was my turbulence fear really just as nutty as the Wings People's fear?

Despite the drawbacks of that class, it did spur me to fly a few times, but after September 11th it was easy to convince myself that my fears had been well-founded, even though, a reasonable person might point out, I was not afraid of terrorism. My anxieties got worse during this period. I stopped taking the subway. I was going to school at Columbia (West Side, 116th Street) and living in the East Village (East Side, 7th Street). The bus ride took two hours, and included two transfers. I could have traveled to Philadelphia in less time. Eventually the massive inconvenience of my fear triumphed over the fear itself and I started taking the subway again.

My not flying probably felt like a personal failure for my father, who was always giving me flying-related self-help books. One of them, *Freedom to Fly*, was published by New Harbinger, a small publisher of self-help manuals with whom he had developed a series called Instant Help. Reading these books helped me to a point, in that they gave me information and statistics. They made me feel better about flying but did not lead to actual flying.

At my father's urging, and because I was writing this book, I finally signed up for another fear-of-flying group. Self-help promises the chance to overcome serious obstacles such as addiction, phobia, and codependency. These problems are unique in that they come from you, and overcoming them is a matter of you vs. you. But is this possible without years of hard work and professional assistance from teams of therapists? Is it possible at all? Can a fear of flying be overcome in just six weeks?

This was how, in 2009, I ended up at the Westchester County Airport with a bunch of other nervous freaks.

"Can I close this door? A lot of people don't like the idea of having doors closed. Will anyone here be uncomfortable if I close this door?" asked Dr. Martin Seif, the associate director of the Anxiety & Phobia Treatment Center at White Plains Hospital. He was in his fifties, with graying hair, a graying beard, and an energetic, bright demeanor. His voice was loud and confident and tinged with humor. When he spoke, he gesticulated dynamically and his body bounced up and down. I was one of about twenty-five students (or patients) at the first meeting of Freedom to Fly, which met weekly at the Westchester County Airport over a period of six weeks.

Dr. Seif continued, "I became a psychologist to try to cure myself. I had lots of phobias, lots of anxieties, lots of panics. I was too terrified to fly for the first half of my life. I am now a very comfortable flyer. I fly whenever I can. I actually like to fly. I love to fly. I want you to learn a lot about flying, because believe it or not, anxiety loves ignorance and the less you know about flying, the more room there is for your imagination to think of horrible things that can happen."

Dr. Seif asked us how many of us had been through security in the last year, not including today.

"In an airport?" someone asked.

I thought this was a fair question; phobics are nothing if not precise.

"Yeah, in an airport, where did you think I meant?" He rolled his eyes. "At an airport."

Only a few hands rose, mine not among them.

I had arrived at the airport two hours before the class—I habitually arrive early, especially when nervous. Having not been in an airport since 1999, I remembered them as dingy, crowded, and having the ambiance of a hospital waiting room (another place you wait for death). I was surprised by how clean and new the airport looked. Expanses of glass covered the north and south walls. The seats were modern, white leather, and pristine. Flat-screen televisions, showing CNN, punctuated the walls. A small airport that only seemed busy just before and after a flight departed, Westchester County was quiet, with few people wandering around. One convenience store sold magazines, hot dogs, and unappetizing pizzas. A replica of a 1950s diner offered more toothsome fare on the second floor. I parked leisurely, I walked leisurely, and I still had nothing to do for a while.

I found my way to the third floor. In the weeks to come, the third-floor window facing the runway would become my sanctuary. It presented as the least scary floor, probably because it was the farthest from the boarding area. I watched planes take off and land

and waited for one to catch on fire. A disembodied voice reminded us not to accept packages from strangers or leave bags unattended. I had no bags.

Eventually I got bored, and boredom was an improvement over waiting to see which plane would burst into a fireball. Then an exciting thing happened.

All the people who would be leading the class sat down within earshot and discussed the fearful fliers entering into the program. It was my first introduction to the people I'd be seeing every week, as well as an opportunity to eavesdrop. If you've ever been to see a psychologist, or any variety of doctor, you might be familiar with the impulse to read another person's secret notes about you. It would be like, I imagine, being handed a user's manual for oneself. Here are some fragments I overheard:

"Single, claustrophobia, last flight was 2005."

"Very typical claustrophobic . . . very, very."

"This is someone who doesn't think he has a fear of flying, but he just throws up. He has no motion sickness in other situations. I thought that he could use this . . . I gave him some Valium . . . the whole family . . . I visited them, they're big drinkers, he's slim, she's very fat, they're both physicians. I think he's crazy, but they're a wonderful family."

"She's an older woman, she drives to California. Her children are very angry with her."

"Why didn't she take the train?"

"There's also a train issue. She's on Lexapro and Klonopin. She's *very* feisty."

"He's an attorney, no meds, very nice young man."

Suddenly, I heard my name. Even though I could hear every

word they spoke about others, it seemed to me they had started whispering. I heard "unmarried, writer, claustrophobic." As a summary of my entire being, it was disheartening. Then they started laughing.

"A zoologist and a professor. Heights, bridges. He'd like to go to India."

"Twenty-eight, product developer, single, she overabused medication."

Finally they walked downstairs, and I followed. I scanned their faces for any sign they had noticed me, but saw nothing. Roughly thirty people assembled by the check-in area: young mothers, a few men, women in business attire. Their ages ranged from eighteen to late sixties. Nobody looked outwardly terrified or strange. We all received name tags and had our parking tickets validated, banal and transactional activities that belied any unease. But the illusion of professional nonchalance was soon broken. A young woman (pretty, blond, unsmiling) wearing blue doctor's scrubs leaned close to a man in his forties (spiky hair, Yankees jacket). Referring, presumably, to the "graduation" flight at the end of the six-week class, she said to him, "So, these are the people we're going to die with." It was unclear if this was a joke or a premonition. I decided to sit as far from her as possible.

The logistics of moving a large group of nervous people through an airport were especially challenging. Legitimate travelers—aka people who were going somewhere—stared at us, no doubt wondering who we were and what we were doing and why we were wearing name tags in an airport. We were instructed to remove our shoes, causing discombobulation among those of us who had not flown since the thwarted shoe bombing of 2001.

Official people checked our names and IDs against an official list.

Then a wonderful man named Tito introduced himself. I had an instant fondness for Tito. He had a mustache, and resembled a 1970s teenage heartthrob. Moreover, he was smiling at us without judgment, kindly escorting us through the airport, tolerating us. He led us outside to a building for employees only. We walked up several dark flights of stairs until we came to a locked door. The claustrophobes started freaking out, some of us quietly, some loudly. Wonderful Tito brandished a key card like a knight with a sword. We spilled into a classroom with a large whiteboard, fluorescent lights, and yellowing motivational posters. One said SAFETY FIRST! and had a picture of an advancing tiger on it.

The counselors assisting Dr. Seif were all former patients of the clinic. One by one, they introduced themselves, citing what they used to be afraid of: driving on parkways, crossing bridges, eating in restaurants, leaving the house. They all described themselves as "ninety-nine and nine-tenths recovered." Betty, who would soon be my counselor, said, "My day started with 'what if' and ended with 'what if,' and now I have learned to not be afraid anymore."

Dr. Seif jumped in: "I didn't fly, as I mentioned, for the first thirty years of my life. I was afraid of heights, afraid of panic, afraid of going too far away, and I was somewhat claustrophobic. I really thought when I was growing up that there were several things I'd never do: I'd never play center field for the Yankees, I'd never play center for the Knicks, and I'd never fly in a plane. It just didn't seem like a possibility.

"Everyone knew I was phobic. I remember in graduate school I was at a party, and I was out on a balcony and someone said, 'I can't believe it, you're doing really well on a balcony on the sixth floor.' I said, 'It's three years of therapy and six drinks.'"

Everyone laughed.

"I'm not kidding. That's really what did it."

During the period when he didn't fly, Dr. Seif took the train whenever he needed to travel. Once, on his way to deliver a paper on phobias, a freak snowstorm caused a long train delay; sitting on the train, he reflected on the irony of his situation. He imagined someone standing at a podium, announcing, *Dr. Seif couldn't be here today to give his paper on phobias because he's afraid to fly.*

Another time he was on a train to Florida with his wife, and the train uncoupled. They were stuck for sixteen hours. At some point, his wife turned to him and said, "I'd rather fly and die than take the train again."

⸻

A phobia is a type of fear that is out of proportion to actual danger, and intense enough to lead to consistent avoidance of the source of that fear. The word "phobia" dates back to 1786, when it was defined as "a fear of an imaginary evil, or an undue fear of a real one." By the nineteenth century, references to phobia were abundant. Dr. M. Roth suggested in 1871 that "people predisposed to extreme states of fear" included "women during periods of catamenia [menstruation], pregnancy, confinement, of secretion of milk and excretion of lochia"; people whose "mental education has been conducted on false principles"; alcoholics; masturbators; and those suffering "sexual excesses." In some cases, he thought, phobia could be hereditary.

Types of phobias are surprisingly manifold. You can have a phobia of chickens (alektorophobia); Bolsheviks (Bolshephobia); beautiful women (caligynephobia); hair (chaetophobia); meat (carnophobia); mirrors (catoptrophobia); teenagers (ephebiphobia); chins and knees (geniophobia and genuphobia); long words (hippopotomonstrosesquipedaliophobia); names (nomatophobia); rain (ombrophobia); everything (panophobia); bald people (peladophobia); beards (pogonophobia); clothing (vestiphobia); and, as they say, fear itself (phobophobia).

Yet psychologist and best-selling self-help author Martin Seligman has argued that "by and large, [phobias] comprise a relatively nonarbitrary and limited set of objects." It is unusual, he points out, for people to have electric-outlet phobias or hammer phobias or chain saw phobias, even though those things pose actual dangers. The top ten fears based on millions of Google searches are, in descending order, flying, heights, clowns, intimacy, death, rejection, people, snakes, success, and driving.

Dr. Seif explained, "If things were totally rational, if we were rational people, we would be most afraid of things that are most dangerous, and least afraid of things that are least risky—that would make sense. But we're not rational. Here's the point: if we look at statistics, it is far safer for us to fly from here to Boston than to drive from here to Boston. Does everyone here believe those statistics?"

The class nodded, almost in unison.

"Occasionally, we get people who don't. But how many people here, if they had the time right now, would get in the car with me and drive to Boston?"

A majority of people giggled and raised their hands.

"See, that's because you don't know me. Right now, how many people could get in a plane and fly to Boston?"

No one raised their hand. I studied the carpet.

"No one," said Dr. Seif. "What we're trying to do together

here, we're trying to figure out why we're far *more* afraid of something that our head says is *less* dangerous and far *less* afraid of something that our head says is *more* dangerous. We're trying to figure out why."

Dr. Seif asked what frightened us about flying and received the typical array of answers.

A petite blond woman raised a fragile hand. "Last time I flew was about four years ago. My fears started shortly after 9/11, but I don't attribute it to 9/11. I landed the day before 9/11. I had been in Europe for three weeks and got back on 9/10. And then 9/11 happened the day after. I'm not afraid of terrorism, but I'm afraid of flying."

"Do you have any other fears?"

"Not that I'm aware of."

"You would be aware of them, unless it was a fear of aardvarks or something. What frightens you about being on the plane?"

"A lot of the things you mentioned. I tend to overthink everything. The biggest fear, I think, is the plane falling out of the sky."

One woman's brother was killed in the towers on 9/11; she wasn't afraid before that. Another woman was claustrophobic. The "very feisty" older woman who regularly drove across the country to see her children said proudly, "[The drive] only takes me three nights." Some people were afraid of panicking, some afraid of dying. Some people were afraid of irony: they would try not to have a good time on vacation to make it less likely the plane would crash.

"One thing that's marvelous about being a human being," explained Dr. Seif, "is that we can have any thoughts we want. You can do whatever you want in your mind and it's perfectly safe. You have a whole different set of rules for what you do in your life. That separation is really important. As we get anxious, the distinction between what we think and what we feel starts to diminish. It's almost like the thought is as dangerous as the action—'Don't think the plane is going to crash!' When we're very anxious, it's very hard to make that distinction."

Dr. Seif turned to a quiet, serene Trinidadian woman. "Why are you here today?"

"I want to overcome my fear of flying."

"When's the last time you flew?"

"Nineteen years ago."

"What a courageous person after nineteen years. Why are you coming here now?"

"Because I feel like I'm imprisoned."

"Didn't you feel like you were imprisoned a few years ago? Why now?"

"I just want to be free."

"Nineteen years ago, you said you flew—was it a scary flight?"

"I think so. My fear increases every year. It goes higher and higher."

"I tell patients, you never forget your first love or your first panic. People can say, 'Nineteen years ago, 1990, I was crossing the street and I got this feeling of panic,' and we do an enormous number of things to avoid it. There's been a lot of research lately that our long-term memory is not fixed. We used to think of long-term memory as essentially on your hard drive. A memory is saved on your hard drive; we grab that memory and bring it back; and we see that memory again. Now we realize that's not the way memory is. Every time you bring up a memory and reexperience it, you change it, and it's that *change* in memory that goes back onto the hard drive. It's really the new enhanced memory, the new anxiety-enhanced memory. I know we can't prove it, but there's a really good chance that nineteen years ago, it wasn't so difficult for you to fly."

After about an hour of discussion, Tito reappeared to let us know a plane was available for us to board. I considered the prospect that their secret plan was to trap us on the plane and take off. I doubt I was the only one thinking this. We walked outside onto the tarmac. It was dark and spooky and no one spoke. We reentered a building and walked to a boarding area. We marched gravely down the extension, as if it were a gangplank on a pirate ship, slower with every step, slowly, slowly. I was one of the first people to board the plane. It was more or less what I remembered, except it seemed a lot smaller, the way one's childhood home, revisited years later, can seem discouragingly minute. It was a "two-by-three," which I later learned means two seats on one side of the aisle, three on the other. Dr. Seif assured us that the plane the class would fly on later would be larger, a three-by-three. That didn't sound much larger, but I was told many times that the extra seat would make a "huge difference."

As soon as the Trinidadian woman stepped onto the plane she burst into tears and keeled over, headfirst, into the front row. Dr. Seif sat next to her and whispered into her ear. "The rest of you, go to the back of the plane," he shouted. We dutifully filed toward the back until we reached the middle of the plane, at which point we all scurried for a seat. We figured that anywhere past the middle of the plane counted as "the back." No one sat in the last row. No one even sat in the last three rows.

I was on the aisle seat of a row of three. Selina, a young mother with a gregarious personality and bright-pink lipstick, sat next to me. We hadn't yet spoken or introduced ourselves when she turned to me and said, "If I say MOVE, you move, because I'm going to be running off this plane."

"Absolutely," I said. "Do you want my aisle seat?"

"No, I'm okay," she said. She whispered to me, "My fear isn't about crashing or height or anything, it's all about . . . I would never go on this flight. Two seats here and three there, there's no air, I just hate everything about it. The ceiling is low . . ."

I smiled. These were my people. We understood each other. After years of hiding our paranoid thoughts we could express them freely and not be judged. I was very aware of a buzzing light, and it started to grow louder. "Is it me, or is that light insanely loud?" I asked to no one in particular. If I had said this to a friend they would have rolled their eyes or looked at me uncomprehendingly.

"It's retarded loud!" shouted a guy across the aisle. We were so happy to agree on this that we practically high-fived.

Dr. Seif walked up and down the aisle, shaking people's seats to simulate turbulence. He shook my seat.

"Do you like that?" he asked. I was surprised by how much I hated it, given that it wasn't that much like turbulence.

"No," I said. "Please stop."

He grinned at me. "You're perfectly safe right now."

"But I don't like it," I said. I knew this was not a particularly sophisticated argument.

Dr. Seif argued with another student, Jeff, who had announced his refusal to participate in the group graduation flight. I also had no intention of taking that flight, but I saw no reason to share that with the class. As I'd been reminded by *The Rules*, getting what you want in the end far outweighs the guilt of dishonesty.

"Won't you keep an open mind about it?"

"No."

"Then why are you here?"

"I want to go to Italy."

"Then why not Boston?"

"The risk is not worth the reward."

"You're not willing to accept the risk of flying for no good reason, is what you're saying."

"Yes."

"I get your reasoning. I know there's the physical chance that every time I cross the street, I could get hit by a car and killed, so I'm not going to go across the street today, because why waste the chance? That's what you're thinking—why waste the chance?"

"Yes."

"If your wife has a flight, do you beg her not to go?"

"No."

"Why not?"

"I don't know."

Dr. Seif sighed. "There is no better use of flying than to be able to say, 'I feel comfortable flying now, I feel as safe as the statistics say I am.' And if you don't challenge that belief with the notion of taking a flight for practicing, then you will never, ever be able to approach that fear. Every time you get on a plane, you'll be walking down a sniper alley with IEDs all over the place and deciding, 'Is it worth it for me to go here, because I might be blown to bits by the time I get to that place.' Unless you allow yourself to reexamine that belief you have . . . the only way to really do it is to open your mind to the possibility that maybe your anxiety is bluffing you, that's all."

"If I was given assurance, I would fly."

"Assurance? Okay, great. But that's not the way life is. Nothing in life is risk-free. But you're willing to drive without assurance. Can you at least acknowledge the fact that you have a different sensitivity to the image of being in a fatal car crash as opposed to being in a fatal plane crash?"

"Yes."

"Even though the end result—your death—is the same?"

"Yes."

"Pleasant thoughts we have here."

A well-respected and influential physician named George Cheyne wrote a very popular book in 1733 titled *The English Malady: or, A Treatise of Nervous Diseases of all Kinds, as Spleen, Vapours, Lowness of Spirits, Hypochondriacal, and Hysterical Distempers, Etc. In Three Parts . . . With the Author's own Case at large.** Cheyne wrote, "Of all the Miseries that afflict Human Life, and relate principally to the Body, in this Valley of Tears, I think, *Nervous* Disorders, in their extream [sic] and last Degrees, are the most deplorable, and, beyond all comparison, the worst." Cheyne had great success with this book, which he wrote intending to make certain aspects of medicine available to nonpractitioners. Unsurprisingly, this was met with hostility from other medical practitioners. Yet Cheyne became something of a cult figure, due to his talent for mixing useful information with inspirational maxims. His books were especially popular among the affluent.

In the eighteenth century, people with phobias were put in asylums alongside those who suffered from much more serious mental disorders. There was no language or methodology to distinguish between different mental illnesses; you were either normal, or you

---

*Cheyne also wrote a dieting book based on his own experience. Before he began his diet he was drinking three bottles of wine a day, and was so overweight that he needed a servant with a stool to follow him when he walked, in case he suddenly needed to sit.

weren't. The result of this lumping together of all mental patients was a stigmatizing of those who had even minor psychiatric illnesses. Those afflicted were said to suffer from moon madness or masturbatory insanity or wedding-night psychosis or old maid's insanity.

In the nineteenth century, George Miller Beard created the diagnosis of "neurasthenia" to describe a disorder that he felt was brought on by the stress of urban life. William James, who had been diagnosed with the ailment, dubbed it "Americanitis." These were words for a phenomenon that was not understood: a disconnect between one's experience of reality and an objective reality, bringing about symptoms of anxiety and depression.

Darwin wrote about an attempt to override his fear response in *The Expression of the Emotions in Man and Animals* (1872). He described coming face-to-face with a puff adder in the Zoological Gardens. A thick pane of glass separated them, and Darwin was determined not to move if the snake struck at him. When the snake snapped forward, however, his resolution disappeared and he "jumped a yard or two backwards with astonishing rapidity. My will and reason were powerless against the imagination of a danger which had never been experienced."

In 1915, Walter B. Cannon, a Harvard professor of physiology, introduced the expression "fight or flight" (originally "fight, flight, or freeze"). Cannon was curious about how our "reflexes favor the continuance of existence." Fear, he believed, was a "foreshadowing of possible injury . . . capable of arousing in the body all the offensive and defensive activities that favor the survival of the organism."

In the 1950s, behaviorist Joseph Wolpe tried to teach cats to fear and love certain stimuli by associating them with electric shocks and food, respectively. Wolpe introduced the still widely embraced notion that relaxation was an antidote to fear—specifically, that if people could be taught to relax their muscles and imagine frightening situations, they might learn to tolerate them. Another behaviorist's approach, on the opposite end of the spectrum, was exposure therapy, known then as "reactive inhibition therapy," "direct therapeutic exposure," or "flooding." While exposure therapy is usually done in manageable doses over a period of time, flooding is a rapid and repetitive exposure to feared objects or scenarios, whether real or imagined. A woman who was afraid of injuring her daughter was asked to imagine jabbing her in the eye repeatedly with a pencil. "Jab, jab, jab!" shouted the psychologist. "You have gone completely crazy." Although this approach caused the mother to cry uncontrollably, after twenty-two sessions she was cured of her fear.

The 1950s were not a good time to suffer from phobias. Psychosurgery, aka lobotomy, was seen as a potential cure. O.T., a fourteen-year-old girl deemed excessively fearful, was lobotomized after nineteen unsuccessful electroshock treatments.

A well-respected lobotomist, Walter Jackson Freeman of George Washington University initially used an ice pick (later called a "stiletto") from his kitchen to perform these surgeries. At one point 63 percent of all US hospitals conducted lobotomies. Estimates on how many people received them range from 20,000 to 35,000. Women were twice as likely to be lobotomized as men, and it was suggested by some that "stilettoing" was most effective in women, Jews, and African-Americans.

Today phobics are treated primarily with cognitive behavioral therapy (CBT), a program of desensitization through gradual exposure. In a *Psychology Today* interview, Fredric Neuman, director of the Anxiety & Phobia Treatment Center in White Plains, described how he would use exposure therapy to cure someone of coulrophobia (fear of clowns). The patient would first be shown pictures of clowns, then presented with a small toy clown. "Ultimately, I'll ask her to dress herself as a clown and to look in the mirror," said Neuman. "She may get frightened, but at least she'll know she's looking at herself."

As part of the $650 fee for the Freedom to Fly class, we were given two in situ sessions with a counselor. I was paired with Betty, a pleasant, trim woman in her late fifties with short, sand-colored hair. She wore a white button-down shirt and a tan jacket. She had green eyes that actually sparkled. She looked so cheerful I worried we wouldn't get along. But as soon as we started talking I liked her.

Betty was a former agoraphobe. She had been so afraid of running into people she knew that she would do all her errands far from her house. She once wore a fake cast on her arm so that she would have an excuse not to participate in local goings-on. When she told me this story I thought she was a creative genius.

At our first meeting at a Barnes & Noble, Betty told me that we would spend our first practice session riding the glass elevators at the Marriott Marquis in Times Square. This made me unhappy, as it involved most everything I don't like aside from flying: crowds, enclosed spaces, heights, Times Square.

"I don't like crowds," I warned her.

"Good," she said in her cheery voice, brandishing her grin like a gleaming weapon. "I don't like crowds either."

A week later we met at the entrance to the Marriott, where narrow glass elevators shot up and down as if on springs. I felt slightly faint.

"Isn't this fun?" she said. "You're lucky I don't make you go on the Ferris wheel at Toys 'R' Us."

"Thanks," I said weakly.

"Do you think you can ride one floor?" she said.

"Sure," I said, feeling uncharacteristically emboldened. "Why not?"

The system of elevator riding at the Marriott is either brilliant or deranged. You press your floor in a central column, and it gives you a letter of the alphabet. You then have to run to the elevator marked with that letter. We missed the elevator several times before finally catching one. We rode one floor up and got off. We summoned the elevator again, and got off after two floors. Finally, I agreed to ride the elevator to the top. As soon as we entered the car, I regretted my promise. Floors passed with alarming speed. Betty tried to distract me with games.

"Name a city that starts with N," she said.

Fear makes you stupid; the brain, occupied with sending panic signals to the body, has little time for higher cognitive function. The ground dropped farther away as we raced upward. I could tell the other people in the elevator really wanted to answer the question for me. They fidgeted with discomfort. I was drawing a blank.

"I don't know. Are there even any cities that start with N?" I said skeptically, forgetting that I lived in one.

After our ride, we walked around the hotel. "I can't believe we can just walk around this hotel and ride the elevators," I said. "The security's not very good. What if we were terrorists?" Betty gave me a pitying look. We rode the elevator downstairs and sat in the food court.

Betty asked me if I had bought a ticket yet for the group flight.

"You know how I feel about crowds."

"There will be other people on the plane no matter what. Won't it be better if you know them?"

"No, it's worse if I know them. I can ignore people I don't know, but people I know I have to pay attention to."

"No you don't."

I pushed on with my multipronged argument, which made perfect sense to me, and only me. "Plus, they'll all be nervous, and that will make me more nervous."

"I think you'll be pleasantly surprised. I think you should get a ticket," she said dismissively.

"What's the flight like?" I asked, trying to distract her.

She laughed. "Everyone from the class is always fine. It's Marty who's a mess. He's more anxious than anyone! He runs around asking, 'What's your level? What's your level?' He drives us all crazy!"

It's not that I didn't feel the class was working; each week my drive to the airport was less terrifying, and each week getting onto the stationary plane was a bit easier. But I still didn't feel ready to fly. I had preemptively decided that the class was just practice; I believed that driving to an airport and setting foot on a plane counted as progress.

Before we parted, Betty informed me gleefully that for our next meeting we would be riding the Roosevelt Island Tramway, the only aerial commuter tram in the country. A glass cabin, it traveled back and forth at sixteen miles per hour, two hundred and fifty feet above the East River at its peak.

"It's near Bloomingdale's!" she squealed, clapping her hands as though this were a mitigating factor.

"Every time I pass that cable car, I think to myself, why would anyone willingly get in a contraption held up by ropes?" By the time I got to "ropes" my voice had jumped an octave.

"Jessica, those are steel cables." Betty said my name only when I was acting obtuse.

"Oh." I really had thought they were ropes. "Are you sure?"

"Yes."

"Don't you think they look like ropes?"

"Not really."

———

We met the next week at Bloomingdale's. I was glum about the whole thing, as one reasonably would be when marching to one's death. "I do this all the time," she assured me. "It's perfectly safe." On the way to the tram we passed Stephen, another classmate, and Alison, another counselor.

"Oh, hi!"

"Did you ride the tram? How was it?"

"It was great!"

"We're just on our way now!" said Betty, dimpling.

It amused me to think there were terrified adults all over the city taking the subway one stop, riding the tram just to turn around and go back, stepping into an elevator with no purpose, stalking the Ferris wheel in Toys "R" Us.

We arrived at the tram. The car looked to be about a hundred square feet. There were a few seats, and poles for standing passengers. I confirmed that it was indeed held up by steel cables. Or, wait, could they be painted to *look* like steel? Either way, I wasn't any happier about setting foot on the tram.

"We'll just sit here and watch it for a while."

"Let's get it over with."

"Do you want to talk to the conductor?"

"No. He doesn't seem drunk."

"I'm sure he's quite sober. I've taken the tram so often, people know me, and the Marriott employees probably think I work there."

We stepped on the tram. I wrapped my whole body around a pole, thinking that this would stabilize me if the tram fell. More people stepped on. Supposedly the tram was built to hold a hundred and twenty-five people (I had actually looked it up) but realistically I knew I would be uncomfortable with more than fifteen. I prayed that the doors would close before it got too crowded. The tram swayed side to side in the wind. Betty saw the look of terror on my face and said, "The tram has to give a little, if it didn't it would break."

All I heard was "tram" and "break."

But it was a short trip. The view over the river was stunning. Roosevelt Island, formerly known as Welfare Island, had been home to a number of asylums (including the Women's Lunatic Asylum, which had an entrance called The Octagon), a prison, and a small-pox hospital. It was known, at the turn of the century, as a place where they sent those too sick to return to society. Somehow, this seemed appropriate to my current circumstance. Now it is a residential community, and many of these old buildings are in ruins.

From where Betty and I landed, you couldn't see any of the ruins. We walked down to the river on the east side and sat on the grass. It was one of the first warm days of spring. Nascent yellow flowers poked through the ground. It seemed like a conspiracy to reassure me that everything was safe and happy and okay. Betty's son called and she excused herself. While I waited, I picked idly at blades of grass and daydreamed about what it would be like to have Betty as a mother.

Back on the Manhattan side, we said good-bye.

"Okay, I have to go do tunnels," she said. "Do you like tunnels?"

I made a sour face and lowered my voice. "Nobody likes tunnels."

Over the next few weeks we met a pilot, whom we barraged with diverse but equally preposterous catastrophic scenarios. We sat on what looked like the same plane every week. A few people disappeared. I was eventually persuaded to buy a ticket. At the end of the six weeks the class met at a new airport for our graduation flight. I had taken an anti-anxiety medication and felt calm. I had often wondered if taking a pill would prevent me from thinking I was about to die on a plane or prevent me from caring. It was the latter.

But, as often happens in travel, all did not go according to plan. Fog delayed the flight. Then the flight was canceled. The group gathered around Dr. Seif, some discouraged, some annoyed, some relieved. We weren't all able to get tickets together on the next flight. I happily volunteered to sit this one out. Dr. Seif said, "This is not the group experience I wanted. We're going home."

I cheerfully gathered my things. I was a good distance from the group when I heard someone shout, "Wait." Tickets had become available for all of us on the next flight. Most people stayed. I left. I walked out with two other women, one of them crying. Sarah, a doctor, told me she was disappointed in herself. I told her she had been brave to come at all, which I meant earnestly. Leaving the airport may have seemed like a failure, but to me it felt like progress. I told her I'd be coming back the next week to try again, and that she should join me.

As I drove to the Westchester County Airport for our last class, I felt a little peculiar knowing we would be discussing a flight I hadn't taken. Most were elated. Usually our conversation revolved entirely around different ways we might die; today, it seemed relaxed and happy. Dr. Seif chimed in excitedly, "The good feeling, the strong feeling, comes from the realization that you have a capacity beyond what you believed."

But not everyone felt good or strong. Bradley, a zoologist, was quite hard on himself. He said, "I thought to myself, there's a 93 percent success rate for overcoming fear, and there's only one person here that's not feeling good, and that's me." Looking dejected, he told us he had brought his "tools" (games and other distractions), but that he had been so anxious he couldn't lift up the tray table and take them out of his bag. His anxiety literally froze him. The thought of this kind, gentle man knowing that something by his feet could help him but being unable to grab it just about broke my heart.

Sarah, Betty, and I met at the airport the following Saturday morning. We boarded a 9:15 flight to Boston, had a bagel in the Logan Airport food court, and flew back on a 12:15 flight. As we boarded the first flight, we saw it was nearly empty. Betty asked if we wanted to meet the pilot. Sarah, who looked green, declined. I reacted like an excited five-year-old. The next thing I knew I was sitting in the pilot's seat, wearing his hat, and he was taking my picture with my cellphone. I asked if I could have one of those wing pins, but he said they didn't have those anymore.

Now that we were best of friends, the pilot insisted we sit in first class. Betty handed me a candy and told me not to put it in my mouth until she gave me the signal. Wondering if she was insane, I stared at the candy as the plane accelerated. At the moment the wheels left the ground, Betty said, "Go!" I put the candy in my mouth. It was one of the worst things I had ever tasted. My whole face twisted and puckered. I made a whimpering noise. "In a minute, the sourness will go away and it will turn sweet," she said. I wondered why she was torturing me. In a minute, as promised, the candy turned sweet. "We're in the air!" announced Betty gleefully. She had performed a magic trick, which to me was more like a miracle. The plane had taken off, and I hadn't even noticed.

————

It's three years later, and I haven't flown since. I feel less afraid of flying, but given that I haven't actually flown, I'm not sure if I can claim that as a victory.

The class certainly helped me more than any self-help book I'd ever read. Though I was free to leave at any time, social pressure kept me there; if I'd been at home reading, I would have stopped at the first distraction. Second, I appreciated the opportunity to argue with a person—though I have been known to argue with a book, it has never argued back—until I ran out of excuses. Keeping company with similarly fearful classmates was a mixed bag. On the one hand, it was like looking into a very unflattering mirror. On the other, they offered the support of a community, reminding me I was not alone. Mostly, I liked Dr. Seif. He was charming and funny, and he wasn't offering empty platitudes.

I later learned that not everyone felt the same way. Some felt he was too confrontational and too mocking in his approach. A classmate later told me she preferred the self-help books she had read over the class. But the combination of class time and real-world desensitization seemed more effective to me than fire walking or vision boards, tools that made you feel powerful but didn't deliver practical, real-world skills.

I e-mailed a few times with Sarah, the other classmate I flew with, and each time she told me she was still very afraid of flying.

She admired how calm I was on our flight, and even though I explained to her that it was more medication than any force of will, she still seemed envious. As we both became increasingly invested in a narrative in which the other person was doing a better job facing her fear, I pointed out that she'd flown several times since our first flight, whereas I had not flown at all. She insisted that I had achieved more regardless, because she was terrified during each and every flight. We agreed to disagree.

The self is never really finished improving. If you lose weight, you can gain it back. If you become wealthy, you can still lose your shirt. I had achieved my goal of flying, but my real goal was to continue flying, not to go to Boston once and return two hours later. Self-help directs us to specific goals, and we may reach those goals; but everything we achieve is temporary. A constant sense of renewal is what keeps the self-help industry alive, year after year. No matter how satisfied you are with your life, the specter of failure always looms ahead, and there will always be a book to help you through it.

A year after the class, someone hacked into my e-mail account and sent all of my contacts a spam letter soliciting money. "I'm writing you this with tears in my eyes," began the e-mail. That my friends and colleagues might think for a moment I would form that sentence horrified me, but the next part, about how I had been robbed in Rome, reassured me that any recipient would know it was a fake. Most of my friends now knew about my fear of flying. When I wrote people asking them to please ignore the e-mail and to not send any money to the address, most people wrote back saying they knew I wasn't in Rome because, unless some drastic infrastructure had escaped their notice, you still couldn't drive from New York to Italy.

Only Betty—dear Betty—left me a phone message expressing her concern.

"I hope you're okay," she said. "But I think it's great that you're flying."

7

THE SADDEST CAMP
IN THE WORLD

On Grief and Grieving

The reason my father and I almost never talked about my mother, aside from our shared antipathy toward melancholy, was the emotionally complicated way in which she died. When I was too young to understand the truth, I was told that my mother had died in a car accident. I'm not sure exactly when I was told that she had committed suicide. I think I was seven or eight. The car accident story was a partial truth, as she had been in a car accident six months before she died, and it was the official family story that this accident was the catalyst for a number of things that contributed to, but do not explain, her suicide: a period of convalescence, depression, pain, wrong medications, poor treatment, bad timing. You'd probably like to know how it felt to think my mother had died one way, and then later find out that she had died another, more horrible way, a way that by its nature implies intentional abandonment and moral ambiguity and muddled incriminations. Most of all, it felt disorienting; a significant fact in the narrative of my life had suddenly changed. Like most seven-year-olds, I wasn't in the habit of thinking of my life as a narrative, but took it for granted as a singular truth. Truth turned out to be a slippery business.

The official narrative morphed again when I was in college. I had been told that my mother had jumped off a bridge. I had seen suicidal people jumping off bridges in movies; I assumed it had looked something like that. It wasn't something I pictured often, but the image was integral to my understanding of what had happened to her. When I was in college, I learned that she had not jumped off the sort of bridge that traverses water, but an overpass in a park, the vital narrative difference being the presence of hard ground. When a body hits the water, it disappears; when it hits the ground, it doesn't. This detail added a new element of brutality to my mother's death. Once again, the world as I understood it shifted.

I started to feel that my world had multiple realities, and not in the benign way that one is aware of minor subjective discrepancies; hard major facts could change at any time. My mind entered a joint custody, where it sometimes took residence in a normal house, and sometimes lived in a house of inchoate violence and chaos; and regardless of which place my mind was visiting, I experienced a vague sense of having left something essential behind at the other, like a toothbrush.

It's not unusual for families to avoid talking about a suicide; some emotional austerity measures are to be expected. What provided some irony was that my father's profession—psychology—espouses the benefits of expressing emotions. There were many reasons for our silence: protection, denial, cowardice, fear, squeamishness, depression, anger, and love among them. Remembering the dead can be a heartening, palliative process; to me, it felt dangerous. My father and I colluded to maintain a collegial atmosphere, as a defense against the despair that silently threatened to overtake either or both of us at any time. It was important, and appropriate, when I was a child, that everything seem okay. As I grew older, however, the pertinence grew murkier. I no longer needed to be protected from the overwhelming sorrow, confusion, and moral chaos of her suicide, yet we had developed a firm habit of ignoring it. It was no longer clear who was protecting whom. How does one terminate these sorts of deeply embedded, implicit contracts?

There is a picture on my desk of my mother and me when I was a baby. We are on the beach, and I am wearing a dumb-looking hat. I think we are in Cape Cod. My mother is smiling and I appear to be eating sand. All is well: a mother and daughter on the beach on a sunny day. My father was probably behind the camera. Looking at it now, though, regarding the past from the future, the photo takes on an ominous cast. Sometimes I look at that picture and I can't help thinking, *You stupid baby. You don't even know what's coming for you. You'd better wise up.*

Implicit in our rejection of grief and loss was a message of self-reliance. When a parent dies, a child becomes aware of a safety void. The child understands, too early, that its parents are fallible and mortal. If the very people who are supposed to protect you are vulnerable, you should probably learn to fend for yourself.

My faith in the primacy of self-reliance wasn't derived solely from my family culture, where affecting a positive attitude was essential to getting on. I grew up in America, where our high regard for self-reliance is not just a matter of taste. We are a nation whose founding document is called the Declaration of Independence. The self-made man epitomizes the American Dream. The values of independence and self-reliance are binding threads in the ideological fabric of America.

"Nothing can bring you peace but yourself," wrote Ralph Waldo Emerson. "Trust thyself," he wrote, inspiring a hundred years' worth of high school yearbook misquotes. Emerson's essay "Self-Reliance" (1841) is a rallying cry for the church of the self. Listening to others, he posits, is a kind of death. It's impossible to read this essay without feeling your breast swell; the notion that you hold so much power is intoxicating. Reading Emerson telling you that you are special, that everything you need and want is within your power and hence your grasp, feels good. To my mind, which is steeped in an ideology that Emerson helped shape, it just sounds right.

Henry David Thoreau and Emerson were close friends; Thoreau's Walden Pond cabin, a physical paean to independence, was built on Emerson's land, a fact you could be snarky about if you wanted. Thoreau's cabin is among the most romanticized pieces of architecture in American history. When my high school English teacher spoke about it, he was misty-eyed (perhaps wishing he were there, and not in a classroom of belligerent high schoolers). But I maintain that few among us haven't at some point wanted, like Thoreau, to go live in a cabin and not need other people. My father was fond of voicing the old adage "If you want something done right, do it yourself." In my experience, that's mostly proven true. On the downside, you end up with a society that values things "done right" over, say, functional relationships.

"Discontent is the want of self-reliance; it is infirmity of will," wrote Emerson. This sounds auspicious, but how true is it? Does it follow that self-reliance brings contentment? If self-reliance is such a cure-all, what happened to my mother? Was her will simply infirm?

By all accounts, my mother was not a lifelong depressive. She was born into a well-off family, was pretty, smart, and outgoing. She graduated from Barnard, sang opera and acted, made friends easily. Maybe things came too easily to her. According to my father, she showed no signs of depression until she was in a car accident at age thirty. She was not critically injured, but her personality seemed to change. She refused to get out of bed. She was given medication for her depression, but it only seemed to make her worse. (It was 1979, and psychiatric medication was more sledgehammer than scalpel.) She began saying that she was a burden, that we would be better off without her. I was one year old.

The day my mother died, my father was at work. She called him several times throughout the morning, which was unusual. She wanted to know if my father had heard from his agent about his self-help book, which he had recently completed. She didn't seem distraught or in danger. My father believes she wanted closure to an open question—Would my father be able to sell his self-help book? Would we be okay?—before she killed herself. The irony presumably escaped her, or perhaps seemed irrelevant. She never did find out.

She left me a birthday present. (My second birthday was in ten days.) It was carefully wrapped. In her suicide note, she suggested that my father marry a single friend of hers who she thought would be a good wife and mother to me. I never saw this note, though I made some half-assed attempts to track it down before I was overwhelmed by a familiar adolescent ambivalence.

I'm telling you her story as if I know what happened, but I

don't. I was there, but I wasn't. This story is a composite of stories that were doled out to me in meager bits over thirty years, fragments that have been eroded by memory, trauma, and denial. When I preface a fact about my mother with "By all accounts," this is not just a rhetorical cliché. All I have are accounts.

It bothers me that my mother's death is an unknowable event. I was the only person deeply affected by her death who wasn't old enough to know what was going on. An almost-two-year-old has no concept of death, even if she experiences the loss of a parent. It has frustrated me at times that the only way I can gain access to my mother's life or death is through other people and their (subjective, biased) memories.

If I'd grasped but cursory information of her life, I understood even less about grieving her death. I had been taught, indirectly, to persevere. Grief seemed like the opposite of perseverance. My insistence on going it alone led me to some bizarre notions. For instance, I worried about dying at thirty-two, the age my mother had been when she died. (I later found out she had died at age thirty-one, another detail I had not known and had denied myself the opportunity to fact-check.) It was a thought that had occurred to me many times, yet it was so irrational that I was embarrassed to tell anyone. I didn't know how I was going to die, but the following scenario was a possibility: out of nowhere, I would become possessed by a mad desire to kill myself, at which point I would leap off the nearest bridge.

This fear dissipated at age thirty. Self-help books, I discovered firsthand, provide the information offered by a community without the hassle of human contact. I had avoided cracking the cover of *Motherless Daughters: The Legacy of Loss* for months. It sat on my shelf: sentimental, threatening, beige. Sometimes I would actually glare at it. I had a number of objections to the book, beginning with the title.

"Motherless." Just slightly preferable to "armless" or "head-less." Part of the way I'd coped with losing my mother was to deny that it had been a loss. I had transmuted a feeling of loss into a feeling of superiority.

The back cover was worse: "A courageous journey into the heart of a woman's most profoundly life-altering passage." I didn't want to make a courageous journey into the heart of anything. I didn't want to be told that tragedy was profound or meaningful. I hated the euphemistic phrase "life-altering passage." Did my revulsion toward words like "nurturing" and "exquisite separateness" smack of defensiveness? Sure. But knowing that did little to mitigate my extreme allergy to them. The publisher also claimed that I would learn "what the unmothered woman can do to reclaim her autonomy *and* restore her connection to the family motherline."

Unmothered? Motherline? It was an embarrassment to the English language. Those weren't even *words.*

So it is with the shame of having literally judged a book by its cover that I admit I was helped by reading this book. Not only was my fear normal, I learned from author Hope Edelman, it was so common that it had an official-sounding name: the parental trigger. "A girl who at a young age loses a mother," writes Edelman, "also loses the ability to perceive herself growing into old age. . . . Instead of envisioning herself as a matron of seventy-three, the daughter then sees early demise as a potential—or even inevitable—physical future for herself." Ninety percent of women whose mothers committed suicide, I learned, fear the same will become of them. I felt, in some small yet consequential way, I had escaped a death sentence.

Edelman writes that after her mother died, she turned to the library:

> I was a reader, and in lieu of a support group or teen-grief therapy, neither of which existed in my town in 1981, this was my best option for support. I needed information. I wanted to know how you were supposed to feel at seventeen when your mother had just died. I wanted clues for how to think about it. How to talk about it. What to say. I wanted to know if anything, ever, would make me feel happy again.

Edelman didn't find that book. She did find an Anna Quindlen column about the death of Quindlen's own mother. Reading about someone else's equivalent experience comforted her so much that, transferring that feeling onto the physical object, she carried the column around in her wallet. That it was not intended as a self-help product did not prevent her from using it as such. In content (if not form), it provided the same comfort as reading an anecdote in *Chicken Soup for the Soul*, or doing a breathing exercise before boarding a plane.

Joan Didion writes in *The Year of Magical Thinking* about turning to books after the death of her husband: "Information was control. . . . I learned from [professional literature on bereavement] many things I already knew, which at a certain point seemed to promise comfort, validation, an outside opinion that I was not imagining what appeared to be happening." C. S. Lewis (best known for his *Chronicles of Narnia*) authored a slim volume in 1961, *A Grief Observed*, after the death of his wife. Madeleine L'Engle, whose husband had died, wrote in my edition's foreword that "reading *A Grief Observed* during my own grief made me understand that each experience of grief is unique. There are always certain basic similarities:

Lewis mentions the strange feeling of fear, the needing to swallow, the forgetfulness. . . . I am grateful to Lewis for the honesty of his journal of grief, because it makes it quite clear that the human being is allowed to grieve." In a society so focused on happiness and progress, grief isolates you and places you out of sync. Can an inanimate object like a book really reunite you with a community, real or imagined, where your experience is normalized?

Lewis himself questions the usefulness of his journal of grief.

> Aren't all these notes the senseless writhings of a man who won't accept the fact that there is nothing we can do with suffering except to suffer it? Who still thinks there is some device (if only he could find it) which will make pain not to be pain. It doesn't really matter whether you grip the arms of the dentist's chair or let your hands lie in your lap. The drill drills on.

Lewis's book is a powerful and complex chronicle of life and death, the profound isolation after a loss, and the difficult if not impossible path the griever faces to reintegrate himself in a community uninterested in discussing absence.

In contrast, it's hard not to see the mere existence of the book *Grieving for Dummies* as an emblem of just how meager the offerings of the self-help industry can be. Aside from the insulting title, the very first line reads, "Here you are holding this book, so maybe you're not a dummy after all."

Maybe?

It continues: "Different parts of the world look at this unsettling fact [that everyone dies], well, in lots of different ways. But one thing is sure: Loss is here to stay as long as you stick around for this wild ride we call life. So one of the things that is real too is this stuff called grief. Though this fact is far from universally acknowledged, I'm here to tell you that grief is a natural, universal response to loss."

Aside from the nails-on-a-chalkboard syntax and the apparent lack of an editor with a basic handle on grammar ("so one of the things that is real too is this stuff called grief"), the casual tone is belabored: unless you're an alien or seven years old, you've probably heard of grief, and the author acting like you haven't is patronizing and mystifying. (Later that page: "This grief thing is doable.")

Ultimately, if I really grit my teeth and see past the language and the reductive graphical sidebars, I can admit that this is a passable book. There's no egregious misinformation; I just don't like the way it's delivered. Flipping to the back of the book, I read that the author, Greg Harvey, is trained in bereavement counseling, and as such is qualified to advise others on this subject. I do find it odd that, according to his bio, he also wrote *Excel for Dummies* and *The Origins of Tolkien's Middle-earth for Dummies*.

Comfort Zone Camp, a grief camp for kids aged 6–18, was started by a slight blond woman named Lynne Hughes. Hughes is not a professional counselor, although she does employ them to help with parts of the camp's programming. Warm and often smiling, Hughes nonetheless has a ghostlike, removed quality. When she was nine, her mother died. No one talked about her mother's death; she and her brothers were expected to go on as normal. Her grandparents moved in with them. Hughes was afraid to go to sleep at night because she thought someone might die. She started having panic attacks, though she didn't know what they were, and neither did anyone else, including her doctor.

Things continued to go downhill. Her father died. Her new stepmother sued her and her brothers for the inheritance. Her brothers acted out. She moved in with her aunt, where she wasn't much happier.

Hughes met her husband as a camp counselor, and after some time doing other work they decided to start a grief camp. She has also published a self-help book for teens about grief, called *You Are Not Alone*. Hughes writes in her book,

> I wanted to catch kids during the grief process and let them meet others who had experienced a significant death, and see firsthand that they weren't alone. I wanted them to be around people who were comfortable being around death and grief and remembering lost loved ones. I wanted to create an environment I hadn't found— but had certainly longed for—after the death of my parents.

I was curious that such a place could exist, and how it could be anything other than a black hole of sadness. Would I even have wanted to go to a camp like this had I been given a choice?

I sent the camp an e-mail, and the PR director called me minutes later. Stacey, the bubbliest and most energetic person I had ever spoken to, invited me to attend one of their camps. But first, she said, I would have to attend a training session for volunteers, even if I were just coming to observe.

The bereavement camp training session was in a town called Livingston, New Jersey, the first of many incongruities I would encounter that day. It was a gorgeous spring day, and right outside the library was a soccer field full of energetic teens. Even Maggie Harrison, who ran the New Jersey branch of the camp, laughed about it: "It's noon on a Saturday and it's 85 degrees outside and we're talking about death and children."

Harrison was one of those people who seemed to have an unlimited supply of pep and energy, as if she had a backup generator in her purse, or was secretly plugged into the wall. She was a true extrovert in every sense, athletic and pretty, with practical shoulder-length brown hair. She didn't walk; she bounced. Harrison told our group of thirty or so potential counselors that she had lost her little brother three years ago. I was surprised to find out that everyone there had lost someone, but of course that made sense: why would anyone think about death in their spare time if they didn't have to?

The New Jersey camp started in 2001 after 9/11, beginning with minicamps for the children who had lost parents. A few years later, they expanded the camps to include all loss: "Murder, suicide, cancer, heart attack, you name it." A sample application was handed out to us. The fictional applicant's name was filled out as "Elliott Smith." I wondered if they knew there was a well-known singer with this name who'd killed himself. The form asked questions such as who died, what relation, cause of death, where they died, whether or not the child was present, if the child had attended the funeral, and if they'd had any professional support. We went over a camp schedule. The first dinner together, Harrison told us, was known as "the awkward dinner."

Harrison introduced Kim Kaufman, a grief counselor who led what they called "Healing Circles." Healing Circles looked to me exactly like group therapy: children and an adult to guide them sat in a circle and talked. While most of the staff were untrained volunteers, the Healing Circle Leaders were all licensed social workers, therapists, or counselors with training in bereavement (though they were also unpaid volunteers). "Kids—especially the little ones— will come up to you and say, 'Who died?' 'How do you feel about that?'" Kaufman warned us. "You need to be prepared if you have a personal loss. You'll hear some tough stuff that nobody should have to experience, least of all a child."

Kaufman's own father had died when she was nineteen. Her seven-year-old brother had made fifty dollars selling tissues at the funeral. She told us this behavior was normal. "In younger children, grief comes and goes."

Sometimes, she said, the kids will tell a story about how a parent died that you know isn't true. She urged us to respect the child's "need to present information" in any way. "All kids are different," she said. "Some of the oldest souls I've met are seven years old."

Harrison turned out the lights and started the promotional video for the camp, a montage of kids playing and having fun, interspersed with testimonials from the children talking about how much it meant for them to have somewhere to go where they could be understood and accepted. Then they showed a clip from the end-of-camp memorial service, a tight shot of a six-year-old boy, who spoke so softly you almost couldn't hear. His face contorted from the effort of trying to speak without crying. He whispered, "In memory of my mother." The *m*'s in the sentence made his mouth twist every time he struggled to open his lips and release another sound. He looked tortured. The whole room burst into tears.

Harrison passed out boxes of Kleenex and promised we would "drink the Kool-Aid and keep coming back."

Despite all the crying, it had been cathartic. I felt light and almost joyful. Feeling uncharacteristically social, I gave a ride home to twin sisters who were liturgical dancers. They spent the hour-long ride patiently trying to explain to me exactly what that is.

Best practices for grieving have long been dictated, yet prescriptions run the gamut from ignoring it entirely to stipulating ritual dress and behavior over a period of several years. In 1671, Simon Patrick, an English theologian and bishop, wrote *A Consolatory Discourse to Prevent Immoderate Grief for the Death of our Friends*, a book so unsympathetic toward the bereaved that I wondered if "consolatory" had a different meaning in the seventeenth century. I looked it up; it didn't. Patrick argued that death was inevitable and common, and thus should not be overly indulged. He wrote,

> Is death such a strange and unusual thing that we should take it heavily? Are your friends the first that ever died? Are you the only persons that God hath singled out to be left alone? . . . A friend is dead. There is one man less in the world than there was. O wonderful! What a prodigy is this! One that was born to die, is dead! It had been a wonder indeed, if he had not died.

But, Simon Patrick, surely some lost lives are worth grieving for—say, the life of an innocent infant? No, says Patrick, referring to human babies with the pronoun "it": "We were once content without it; why cannot we be content without it now? It never loved us, nor was capable to show any affection to us, and therefore we may the better part with it."

Benjamin Grosvenor's *The Mourner: Or, The Afflicted Relieved* (1765) allows grievers some emotion, admitting that "Jesus himself wept over Lazarus; which he would not have done, had there been anything unseemly in dropping a tear over a departed friend." Still, much of the text outlines the detriments of excessive sorrow. As the title suggests, grief is an "affliction," not part of a healthy process. Grosvenor advises readers to turn their complaints and prayers to God, because "my friends are quickly weary of my complaints: it is burdensome to them, though it relieves me." He also suggests that we imagine our own deaths and the deaths of our friends daily, so as to be better prepared for those inevitable ends. The advice must have been useful to some, as the book was rereleased a hundred years later under the title *The Afflicted Man's Companion.*

Views of mourning as a superfluous and even gauche pastime continued through the next two centuries. Many argued death should be regarded as a blessing, since it meant passage into Heaven. Songs and poems about death in the nineteenth century had titles like "'Tis All Bright Beyond, Grandma." In religious children's periodicals, stories about death were used to proselytize. (The infant mortality rate at this time for white children was around 20 percent; for black children around 34 percent.) The *Children's Friend* and *Little Gleaner* carried regular features depicting the last moments of dying children. In these numerous deathbed scenes, the emphasis was placed on a release from earthly suffering and the beginning of a joyous reunion with God. Several of the magazines had a regular feature called "Juvenile Obituaries," which listed "virtuous" children who had recently died. Take, for example, brave Little Robert, a consumptive, in 1837:

> His patience was wonderful for so young a child. Though full of sores, he was never heard to utter a complaint, and often while his Mother expressed her surprise at his fortitude, while his bones were

literally piercing through his tender skin, he would meekly observe, 'Oh! This is nothing to what my dear Saviour suffered for me.'

In 1835, Benjamin Rush, one of the signers of the Declaration of Independence and a professor of medical theory, wrote on grief in *Medical Inquiries and Observations Upon the Diseases of the Mind*. Treating grief as though it were a disease, he outlined physical symptoms of grief and offered curatives, including opium and bloodletting. Rush listed the symptoms as

ACUTE
insensibility
syncope[*]
asphyxia
apoplexy[†]

CHRONIC
fever
wakefulness
sighing (with and without tears)
dyspepsia[‡]
hypochondriasis
loss of memory
gray hairs
marks of premature old age in the countenance
catalepsy
madness

---

[*]fainting, swooning
[†]sudden paralysis or stroke
[‡]indigestion

Rush claimed that grief sometimes brought on sudden death without any symptoms of former disease. Autopsies of those that had "died of grief" showed congestion and inflammation of the heart, he noted, "with a rupture of its auricles and ventricles"; they died of a broken heart.

Rush recommended opium (to be "given in liberal doses in its first paroxysm, and it should be repeated afterwards, in order to obviate wakefulness"); the "discharge of tears"; and "bleeding and purges" for those who show "symptoms of great excitement." Further, he advised that the grief-afflicted should not be allowed in the room where the deceased expired, nor should they see the corpse or the grave. After the initial weeks of mourning, a ban on the name of the deceased (or anything that might revive memories of the dead) should begin; however, "the appearance of mirth and even cheerfulness, should be avoided."

Emily Post's etiquette book in the 1920s included a chapter on grieving. After a lengthy description of fabrics that are or are not acceptable for mourning attire, she instructs that babies should not wear black because it is "too pitiful." Elisabeth Kübler-Ross introduced the popular and enduring concept of the "five stages of grief" in 1969. These stages originally applied to hospice patients and were known as the "Five Stages of Receiving Catastrophic News." By the time her book *On Death and Dying* was published she had changed their name to the "Five Stages of Death and Dying." The now-familiar stages—denial, anger, bargaining, depression, acceptance (DABDA)—were originally intended to describe the reactions of a terminally ill patient, and not of a bereaved person left behind. That fact was lost to most readers, and even more so to people who heard about the "stages" by word of mouth. Kübler-Ross became so famous for her bestselling book that she was named a *Ladies' Home Journal* "Woman of the Decade." In part due to the overwhelming interest in her book, thanatology (the study of death) and dolorology (the study of pain) became legitimate academic disciplines.

There is quite a bit of controversy over Kübler-Ross and her topography of grief. I found more than one article angrily debunking DABDA, where you could practically feel the venom dripping off the page. DABDA had a persuasive monopoly on Western culture's understanding of grief for decades. Now, however, most grief theories have rejected part or all of the Kübler-Ross model. Some have argued there are four stages instead of five; some believe that they can happen in any order and multiple times; some have named different stages altogether; some don't believe in stages at all; some refer to them as "cycles" or "tasks."

In her follow-up book, *On Grief and Grieving*, EKR herself admits that "the stages have evolved since their introduction, and they have been very misunderstood over the past three decades. They were never meant to help tuck messy emotions into neat packages. They are responses to loss that many people have, but there is not a typical response to loss, as there is no typical loss. Our grief is as individual as our lives."*

A few weeks after my training session, I packed for grief camp. My father called to remind me to bring bug spray and sunscreen.

---

*Later in her career, EKR started experimenting with mediums and séances and was involved in a scandal at her retreat in Escondido, California, where a self-proclaimed "spirit medium" often had sex with widows, claiming to be possessed by their dead husbands.

Remembering the little boy's face from the promotional video, his mouth screwed up while he tried not to cry, I contemplated packing several boxes of Kleenex. Then I remembered that I had asked Maggie about bringing Kleenex at the training session. She'd laughed. "God no. They're part of our basic supplies. We order cartons of them!"

Unlike the sunny training day, my drive to the camp was plagued by hard, pounding rain. When I arrived, my name was checked off a list and I was handed a remarkable amount of stuff: a name tag that also functioned as a purse to wear around my neck, waivers to sign, two Comfort Zone Camp T-shirts (they read SPONSORED BY NEW YORK LIFE on the back, which struck me as uncomfortably predatory), a nylon drawstring sack, a CZC/NY LIFE water bottle, and a schedule. I am a lifelong, pathological list-maker, and believe me when I tell you that the schedule was a masterpiece: events were plotted in one-hour to half-hour increments, with no moments to spare. This fast-paced scheduling was one way that a high-energy, non-despairing experience was achieved. There was literally no time for boredom. There was, however, time for sadness, in the form of Healing Circles: 7:45–9 p.m. on Friday, 11 a.m.–12:30 p.m. on Saturday. I was happy to see that eating s'mores was scheduled for 8–9:30 p.m. on Saturday night (along with "Bonfire/Music").

The site was a regular camp in New Jersey that had been rented by CZC for the weekend. It was a large property, with a swimming pool and lake, and hiking trails and ropes courses threaded through the surrounding woods. There was a mess hall where we ate all our meals, and cabins tucked in between the trees. A particularly scenic path led to a bridge over a river, and then up to a secluded campfire spot, where the Saturday-night memorial service would take place.

At the first staff meeting, before the kids arrived, the energy was mixed. The veteran volunteers were in high spirits; the new counselors were nervous. My Healing Circle Leader was a smiling, bright-cheeked man named Ed. I was surprised to discover that the people at the grief camp were some of the cheeriest people I had ever encountered. Ed gathered the group around and explained to us that the volunteers were called "Bigs" and the campers called "Littles." Immediately, my language hackles rose. (Okay, truthfully, they had already been slightly raised by "Healing Circle." I had previously had several long and troubling discussions with myself about why this was or was not a good name for a group therapy session for children, and what else it could possibly be called that would meet with my stringent and unforgiving and horribly judgy approval, and had failed to reach a satisfying conclusion.) While researching this book, the language of self-help had distracted and annoyed me to such an extent that it began to interfere with my capacity for empathy (see: *Grieving for Dummies,* syntax).

The renaming of things to signify that they belong to a different system is a falsehood of convenience. The new names often function to establish new relationships within a fixed time and place. Children at camp become "campers." Adults and children who are strangers to each other enter an instant relationship when they become "Bigs" and "Littles." Likely no one considered the moniker "mini grievers" or "tiny sads" for the children, although that's also what they were. But that would have been a downer, and the camp was trying to provide a positive, upbeat experience. I will concede that there was a certain accuracy to the naming of the littles and bigs, in that the ones called "Little" were in fact littler than the ones called "Big," the exception being yours truly, who was notably smaller than all but one of the teenaged Littles in our Healing Circle.

Language should reflect truth, not manufacture reality. The Healing Circle was another aspirational renaming. But the activity it referred to did not always feel like a "Healing Circle." Most of the time it felt like a "That Is So Fucked-Up Circle."

The self-help lexicon had also offered me a way to hide. As the daughter of a psychologist and parenting expert, I had learned to parrot the language of emotion. I could talk about feeling sad or scared without having to feel sad or scared. I played my real emotions so close to the chest I couldn't see my own hand.* Conveniently, the vestigial language of self-help I had learned in childhood allowed me to disguise this fact from others. Ready-made phrases offered themselves to me like perfectly wrapped euphemisms I could gift into conversations; variations on the popular "What doesn't kill us makes us stronger" were a favorite. I knew exactly how and when to put a positive spin on my mother's suicide, like telling people how "it had allowed for a very close relationship with my father." When reciting my speech I always neglected to mention my dearth of female friends, my feeling that I was completely alone in the world and entirely responsible for myself, how my ability to endure the most extreme forms of stress was balanced with an inability to handle the most common crises.

Certain forms of lying are socially acceptable. It's hard to imagine that when people asked about my mother they really wanted me to say things like "Yes, it's frightening to be aware of one's own

---

*n.b.: Not a metaphor. My father sold "feelings cards," which were like regular playing cards, except instead of numbers there were feelings.

mortality and essential powerlessness at such a young age," or "It made me realize that I was entirely alone in the world, and that there was nothing I could do to stop people from dying or leaving," or just "Life is bleak." I can't say for sure, since I never said these things, but I'm guessing they'd be conversation stoppers.

Ultimately, helping orphans, no matter what name you called them by, made my stringent lexicographical complex seem morally insignificant. I won't pretend that I didn't still cringe slightly when someone referred to a camper as "my Little," but I did learn to let it lie.

We talked about the arriving Littles. Although all the kids in our group had lost a close family member, the deaths were diverse: two overdoses, one suicide, one heart attack, one ovarian cancer, one car accident. One Big had learned about the camp only two weeks ago, and hadn't gone to a training session. He was nervous, because his camper was unfriendly to him. "My Little said two words to me on the phone," he lamented. I patted him on the back, saying something vague and reassuring, while secretly anticipating for him awkwardness of catastrophic proportions.

Almost every adult there had also lost someone in their immediate family: a sister, a mother, both parents, or a close grandparent. It was like I'd been invited to a secret club. I had a consoling, if macabre, feeling of belonging.

The administration knew I was there as a writer to report on the camp, and I had agreed not to write anything specific about the campers or their stories that would make them identifiable. However, it was also agreed that if the Littles knew I was a writer it would inhibit their sharing, which was the whole point of the camp. So I toed the honesty line: when people asked me what I did, I told them I was a writer, working on a book about self-help, and that some of what I was writing about was grief related. My official position at the camp was "Floater," which meant I was an extra set of hands for whatever needed doing. I helped set up chairs and light candles for the memorial service, or ran small errands and messages between organizers and Healing Circles. I was, however, conspicuously the only Floater who was allowed to join a Healing Circle. A few people sensed something off about my inclusion, and occasionally regarded me with a gimlet eye.

There was a rumor going around that one camper's parents had told him they were going to the beach for the weekend and then had dropped him off at grief camp instead.

"That *sucks*," someone shouted. Everyone nodded, eyes wide.

Ed said optimistically, "Well, we'll try to turn it around for him and hope he has a good experience."

I wandered to my cabin to unpack. Kathy and Lisa, both bereavement counselors, roomed with me in a cabin that could easily have housed twelve. Lisa worked for an organization called Grief Speaks. Kathy worked for the state of New Jersey as a crisis counselor. Both were there to train as Healing Circle Leaders. It turned out Kathy was in my Healing Circle. Soon we were swapping death stories. The tone of our conversation was a cross between soldiers sharing war stories and a kind of morbid gossip. Kathy's sister was murdered in a grocery store parking lot, in front of her own daughter. An angry ex-lover had driven his car into them as they crossed the parking lot, then jumped out of the car and stabbed Kathy's sister to death in front of the giant glass windows of the grocery store. It was a clear Sunday afternoon, and the murder was witnessed by clerks and shoppers. Kathy's niece survived. The grocery store checkout clerks were so traumatized they had to be given grief counseling.

By the time Kathy had finished her story, my mouth was agape.

"How on earth do you recover from something like that?" I asked her.

"I didn't want to see a therapist," she said. "I didn't want someone who hadn't been through what I went through to tell me that it would be okay. You don't *know.*"

But needing someone to talk to, Kathy had joined a group called Homicide Survivors.

"What was that like?"

"It was fun!" she said.

"Fun?"

"Those people had the best sense of humor," she said. "They had to. When I told the group that my sister had been run over and then stabbed, someone said, 'What, because she wasn't dead enough?'"

We met for dinner at 6 p.m., followed by our first Healing Circle. Kids told their stories: a heart attack (witnessed); a father hit by a car while he was bending down to tie his shoe; a long battle with cancer; a suicide. If the teenager was shy about telling their story, we played a macabre version of twenty questions: *Who died? How did they die? How long ago did they die?* I asked a few questions, but mostly kept silent. They talked about what it was like if their surviving parents were dating or remarried. They talked about having to move, because on one parent's or no income they could no longer afford the mortgage—which meant having to leave their friends and memories and familiar comforts, on top of losing a parent.

Some of them cried while they told their stories; others seemed calm and distanced. They expressed anger at their living parents, at their dead parents, at their extended family for not helping out financially. Many of the widowed moms had had to start working.

They talked about things that annoyed them during the funeral, like hugs from strangers. "Like, why are you touching me?" said one girl, laughing and exasperated at the same time. "I don't know you."

While their parents had shown some sense in sending them to this camp, they had also previously behaved in obtuse, astonishing ways. One mother had lied to her son about his father's suicide so as not to upset him on vacation. He came home thinking his grandmother had died, only to find out his father had killed himself.

Their stories were both deeply harrowing and inspiring. I found myself wishing that I had had something like this when I was a kid. While my avoidance may have looked like fortitude to others, it was the easy way out. What's hard is honesty, confrontation, and vulnerability. I had an immense amount of admiration for what these teenagers—who, as a social group, get a bad rap—were doing. Their willingness to cry in front of other people, especially at that age of extreme self-consciousness, was brave.

That night I slept the sleep of the emotionally spent.

Saturday morning came way too soon. At 8:30 a.m., Kathy and Lisa and I stumbled to the cafeteria in search of coffee. There we found sixty hyperactive campers, and seventy-plus adults in need of three hours' more rest and several gallons of caffeine. A man who would become the unfortunate target of my sleepy resentment announced that the group of kids who yelled the loudest would get to eat first.

After lunch I heard more heart-wrenching stories: of long battles with cancer, children who had only ever known their parent as a sick person, who had spent the majority of their childhoods in a hospital. One girl said, "My family wouldn't let me see [my mother]. I was so mad. I fought my way through them so I could stand by her [death]bed." Parents died at home, parents died in hospitals. Two parents died from drug addiction. When the parents were drug addicts or alcoholics, there tended to be some relief, mixed with anger and sorrow.

Saturday night, I walked to the memorial ceremony in a slow processional with the entire camp. Along the path were candles in paper bags, which I had lit earlier as part of my Floater duties. They winked with a warm, soft shimmer. At the site, we gathered around a large bonfire. The kids wrote the names of their loved ones on small pieces of paper and threw them into the fire, saying, "In honor of my mother," or "In honor of my brother."

The faint sound track of bad covers of "Pretty Woman" and "Satisfaction" wafted through the trees; there was a wedding nearby. Two rituals were happening within earshot of each other: one of celebration, one of mourning. Ritual, I was beginning to understand, gives structure to the chaos of life. It tells us how to behave, how to dress. It gives us actions to take. Sometimes it tells us how to feel. Or reassures us that what we feel is acceptable. Ritual helps us to be present and confront reality in a way that feels safe and structured.

A second memorial service for the campers and their parents closed the weekend. Each Healing Circle group was asked to give a presentation for the parents, a sort of grief-themed talent show. A singer from my group had volunteered to sing a song her mother had taught her, and when our group name was called we all shuffled toward the stage. She had a clear and lovely voice, and despite my best efforts at stoicism I started to cry. A fourteen-year-old teenager who was at least nine inches taller than me handed me a box of tissues, and hugged me to her substantial bosom. I felt simultaneously comforted and uncomfortable. It was a generosity beyond the likes of anything I had ever shown for a teenage girl to console a thirty-year-old weeping stranger in front of an audience. In appreciation, I tried to avoid getting snot on her polo shirt.

The final stage of the memorial service was a balloon release, where campers wrote messages to their loved ones and tied them to the strings. We counted backward from ten, and released our balloons simultaneously. While environmentally unsound, it was visually stunning. The balloons rose slowly, big circles of color turning into tiny pinheads of color turning into clear blue sky. It was easy to imagine the balloons were going to wherever the dead people were, whether you believed in Heaven or not.

Sunday night when I got home, I was more tired than I'd been in years, an unusual combination of physical and emotional exhaustion that comes from talking about death and then going on a four-mile hike. My father called to see how it had been.

"What was it like to be around other people who had lost family members at a young age?" he asked.

"It was nice," I was surprised to hear myself say.

My father told me about having a booth at a convention once where he was set up across from a national suicide prevention organization.

"For three days I was staring at a big sign that said SUICIDE. It was starting to drive me crazy. Finally, I went over there. I was shy about it. I said, 'I have a personal connection; what is your group?' It turned out her father had committed suicide. She gave me some pamphlets. I thought maybe you and I could go sometime. The thing is, everyone thinks they're the only one."

I said I would go with him to the group. I also suggested he might enjoy volunteering at the camp. To my surprise, he wasn't interested. He said, "I'm always the counselor. I avoided talking about Ellen's death for a long time."

"You don't want to be the counselor anymore."

"I want to be the patient."

8

NEW FRONTIERS OF WEIRDNESS

The Future of Self-Help

Columbus Day weekend, 2011, my father and I arrived at the AUSA (Association of the United States Army) Annual Meeting & Exposition in Washington, DC, one of the largest military conventions in America. The event slogan, printed on colossal posters, read VOICE FOR THE ARMY, SUPPORT FOR THE SOLDIER. Above these words floated an emblem: a tan eagle in profile, a shield with a torch on it, a crowning laurel. My father was about to introduce his latest self-help product.

The morning of the convention I woke up at 0700 hours faced with the challenge of what to wear. From the lengthy prescriptions about uniforms on the agenda, I guessed that my regular blue jeans would not be appropriate. I had exactly one item of clothing in army-green, a fetching silk blouse, so I threw that on, along with a long black skirt and black high-heeled boots.

I wasn't supposed to be there. As you might imagine, any event associated with the Army is not exactly open to the public. My father had borrowed a plastic ID badge from his colleague, Sandy Collins, which he put around my neck. "If anyone asks, you're Sandy Collins," he stage-whispered.

Once inside, I was surprisingly nervous. I tried not to make eye contact with anyone and walked quickly, with feigned confidence. The ground floor of the convention center had little on it except a few hardy potted plants. A glut of men in business suits and Army uniforms talked on their cell phones, walked with purpose, checked their e-mail.

My father and I rode down an escalator in front of a movie screen showing a commercial for new helmet technology set to Rambo-esque music. It was like entering a violent video game. As we turned a corner into the main exhibition area we were surrounded by life-size tanks, assault rifles, missile launchers, bazookas, biohazard suits, full-body armor, bulletproof uniforms, more tanks, more guns, guys picking up guns and pretending to shoot them (I turned around at one moment to find myself staring down the barrel of a gun), remote-controlled robots, and remote-controlled robots outfitted with cameras and bombs and missile launchers. We passed a mannequin wearing an all-black, all-rubber hazmat suit, where the only exposed part of the human body was a tiny hole around the eyes, nose, and mouth. The suit was too large for the mannequin. Large rubber hand-like objects hung limply by the mannequin's sides, having the eerie effect of an intact human skin with the bones, muscle, and blood siphoned out of it. We passed a sand-colored tank with tires taller than I was. To my right, a tall muscular man with shorn hair talked on his cell phone while leaning casually on a missile launcher. He might have been talking to his wife about dinner, but anything you do while leaning on a missile launcher takes on an outsize drama.

"Wow," said my dad.

"Wow," I echoed.

"Well, this is weird."

"It's like a new frontier of weirdness for you," I agreed. "Congratulations."

"Thanks," he said, I think genuinely pleased.

The room echoed with the muted sounds of a thousand conversations. I tried to imagine what sorts of exchanges might be taking place. *Does this tank come in other colors? How much does this AK-47 weigh?* Surveying the overwhelming scene, I leaned on a large black metal thing until I noticed the sign that said STAY CLEAR. TURRET MOVES WITHOUT WARNING.

My father had been invited by a company he freelanced products for. Military Community Awareness, or MCA, represented the softer side of this convention. With my father's aid, they created products to help Army families deal with challenges like distance, moving frequently, and loss. While a majority of the products for MCA were self-help workbooks, they also had magnets, coloring books, "positive message" bookmarks, and self-help pens. (I had a pen in my bag for several months that read COPING WITH BEING APART; it contained a scroll that, when unfurled, revealed bullet points on the "four stages of separation" and helpful remedial tips.) My father had come up with the concept for these pens, as well as most of MCA's products on various mental health topics tailored for military families. The latest product my father had developed for them was a self-help app. The app part wasn't unusual; apps had recently become the new frontier for self-help, and were accessible to anyone with a smartphone. What was unexpected, for my father anyway, was that the app was for suicide prevention.

Suicide is one of the military's biggest mental health challenges; the military has the highest suicide rate in the US (teens are the second highest at-risk group). My father's app was called "Operation Reach Out."* When he first told me about it, I was surprised. In all of his game-making, book-writing, and toy-creating, he had never made a product addressing suicide. My father had in fact made such a thorough habit of not discussing my mother's death that few of his friends and colleagues even knew about it. Now, he found himself exposed. "At first I didn't tell anyone," he said, "that I had a personal connection." For months, he had worked on the app with colleagues without telling anyone his first wife had committed suicide. When he finally shared his story, he told me, he felt relieved. "It was an important thing for me to disclose."

I had mixed feelings. I was glad that my father was finally facing this consequential event in our lives, and I thought it was a crucial topic to address. However, the idea of an app for suicide prevention seemed insufficient. Even the word, "app," was foreshortened. Suicide seemed too vast, too serious, and too dangerous to be dealt with via smartphone. Apps, in my view, were for playing Sextuple Word Challenge on the subway and checking the weather. But my father disagreed.

"This is the future of self-help," he said. "What's better: a book sitting on a shelf somewhere, or a tool that people will carry with them in their pocket every day?"

---

*Both my father and I tended to refer to it as "the suicide app," perpetuating a lazy habit of truncation that makes self-help so annoying and pernicious.

Technology probably is the future of self-help. There are already smartphone apps to help you with your confidence, your fears, your self-esteem, your weight loss, your optimism. Every self-help program has a website. It's possible, even probable, that someday self-help will be entirely electronic.

A few years before my father created his app, I met an MIT graduate who had created a robotic weight-loss coach. Cory D. Kidd was visiting New York City to meet with some venture capitalists and health care companies (he wouldn't be more specific, nor would he let me come with him to his meetings) to convince them to invest in his robot, Autom. Kidd was young, affable, energetic, and wearing a fancy suit. He had brought with him a prototype from Hong Kong, where he had been living and working with his wife, an engineer.

Autom was part of a class of robots known as "sociable robots," which are programmed to mimic human relations, using skills like eye contact, taking turns, and responding continuously to new data. About fifteen inches tall and weighing five pounds, Autom had a white plastic head with round, black eyes and a pageboy hair helmet. Its head was attached to a sturdy, bread-maker-like torso, which also contained a computer. Autom lacked arms and legs. Kidd was considering, however, adding eyelids. "How much difference does a blink make?" I asked.

"We'll see." He shrugged.

Autom was programmed with a woman's voice, because women, Kidd said, are traditionally seen as more sympathetic. Kidd referred to Autom as "she" when he spoke, a habit I could not quite bring myself to adopt. Autom had a camera behind its eyes that pinpoints the middle of your face, making it seem as though you and the robot are making eye contact. On this occasion, however, Autom's eyes rolled about in all directions as though it had attention deficit disorder, never finding my face. It was disconcerting. Kidd apologized, explaining that the robot had been jostled on the plane and a screw had fallen out.

In 2005, Kidd ran a study with the cooperation of the Boston Medical Center. Autom was programmed with one thousand questions to ask dieters, who would then write their answers on a screen with a special pen. Autom then responded to this data, giving encouragement, suggestions, or praise, or asking new questions.

Robots, it turned out, can be effective self-help aids. Compared with two other groups that used a journal and a computer program, the subjects paired with Autom lost the most weight. The results were propitious, both for Kidd and for dieters. An endlessly duplicable robot coach potentially means more access to help for more people. On the other hand, not everyone is ready for a future where robots help you help yourself. After Kidd dropped off one robot, an unhappy participant contacted him.

"I got a call the next day, and this man said, 'It's not working. You need to pick it up.' I asked, 'Would you like me to come and fix it?' He said, 'No! It's not working!' He hung up on me. I called back later, and said, 'I'll come pick it up; when would you like me to come?' He said, 'I'm not planning around your schedule,' and hung up on me again. So I called back one more time, three days later. I said, 'When would you like me to come pick it up? I will come at your convenience.' He said, 'Come pick it up *now.*' So I drove over to his house. There's the robot, sitting on the front stoop, with the cord tightly wrapped around its neck. He wouldn't even open the door! He talked to me through the window. He said, 'It's coming alive at night and doing things while I'm sleeping.' He was quite serious. When I got back, I looked at the robot log—I had programmed it to record every interaction so I could keep track for the study—and he had never even turned it on."

The "uncanny valley" theory attempts to explain why robots that mimic humans can make us uneasy. If a robot looks ninety-nine percent human, the theory posits, our brains become obsessed with the missing one percent. A robot that looks too much like a human is like "a corpse that moves."

MIT's lawyers initially expressed reservations about the study; concerned that the robot could cause heart attacks or encourage people to commit suicide because it was talking to them about being overweight, they recommended against it. Turning to a self-help book is socially alienating; turning to a robot could be even more so.

Personally, the idea of robot help makes me lonely to the bone. It's self-reliance taken to an extreme. Yes, life is scary and complicated and chaotic and sad-making and too full of information to comprehend, much less process or understand. Yes, self-help whittles that gargantuan mess down to something that seems more manageable. But it's an impoverished life you build, more machine than human. It merely works; it doesn't live.

———

My father had grown up in DC, and I was born at the Georgetown Memorial Hospital. DC was where my father and mother had bought their first, and only, house together. It was a red brick house with a steep grassy lawn in the back. I remember very few things from my early childhood, but I do remember that lawn. At the bottom of the lawn was a short path that led to a stone sculpture-cum-bench in the style of Picasso. The flattened laps of a seated man and woman formed the bench. That small, protected area where the bench sat felt like a magical place to me, an enchanted forest. There is a picture of me as a toddler sitting on that bench, in the lap of the stone couple, wearing purple corduroy overalls, and looking pleased. My arms are outstretched, reaching for something that is not there.

DC is also where my mother killed herself. We used to come to DC at least once a year when my grandmother was alive, but now that she has passed I rarely visit.

Now I had returned to this city to watch my father present an antisuicide app. I returned my badge to its proper owner, Sandy Collins, my father's colleague. She was a trim, well-dressed woman from Long Island who had been with the company for thirteen years. Collins was warm and confident and smart. She radiated professionalism, and seemed annoyed by her and my father's boss, Jon, who had shown up late, forgotten to bring his business cards, and generally seemed distracted and at loose ends. I got the feeling she would have fired him if she could.

The MCA booth had cost $5,000, yet was minuscule compared to the Saab booth, which contained realistic models of planes and missile launchers. Collins surveyed the table of products, which included games and books my father had made. There were laminated flip-books and posters and pens and coloring books and "Handy Hints foldout packs" with information on stress, anxiety, PTSD, sexual abuse, child abuse, traumatic brain injury, coping with injury, depression, alcohol and substance abuse, finance, family communication, grief, and suicide. She frowned. "We need more products on sexual abuse." She turned to my father. "Can you make something on sexual abuse?" Collins turned to me and explained that her contacts at the bases told her what they needed, so she could tailor the products accordingly.

Meanwhile, we were surrounded by guns. I come from a liberal, gun-fearing background. I had never seen a gun up close, and I had certainly never held one. The incongruity overwhelmed: my father at one table, selling mental health products; people at other tables, selling weapons.

Looking around at all the guns I couldn't help thinking of a statistic I'd read: 67 percent of suicides in the Army are by gunshot. How many of these guns might someday be used for this purpose? Other methods of suicide included hanging (19.8 percent) and overdose (4.6 percent). The primary cause of suicide is listed as "relationships," but in 42 percent of cases the primary motivation is unknown. Those trying to help soldiers with their mental health face a number of challenges, the most intractable being fear of stigma: 51 percent of soldiers say they believe simply seeking help for mental health issues would damage their career. Self-help might be the best and only practical option for a soldier dealing with mental health issues.

My father was the only psychologist who worked for MCA; his boss was a businessman whose business happened to be selling mental health products to the Army. Thus, my father's presence was necessary to their professional legitimacy. Whenever someone inquired about the app, Jon would tell them, "It's free. We're giving it away. We appreciate what you do for us and we want to give back," after which he would introduce "Dr. Shapiro," to explain and demonstrate the app.

The app was still in development, and would not be released for another few months. It was also buggy, which irritated Jon, who kept telling my father he needed to "fix that," even though my father was not the programmer. He had a point. This was the rare app where a programming glitch could have lethal consequences.

And it was flawed. When I tested the app on MCA's iPad, I was presented with two options: one button said *I'm concerned about myself*; the other said *I'm concerned about someone else*. I tapped *I'm concerned about someone else*, but it took me to the link that should have followed the other button, and I was presented with questions like *Do you know how you will kill yourself?* Suddenly, I *was* concerned about myself.

Depending on which question you answered, you would be directed to a series of short videos. Tight shots of actors' faces, speaking into the camera, effectively simulated a person directly talking to you. The videos had titles like "There Is Hope," "There Are Other Options," and "Better Times Lie Ahead." The actors, wearing Army uniforms, spoke in short, unambiguous statements such as "Suicide is not the answer to your problems," and "You are not alone." The app also had a place to enter personal contacts, a list of resources like suicide hotlines, and suggestions of activities that would connect you with other people ("go see a movie" or "start a blog"). Like all self-help books, a disclaimer on the very first screen of the app warned that it was "intended as a self-help tool only and is not meant to be a substitute for professional mental health services."

The fact that this particular self-help product was offered without remuneration seemed to alleviate for my father the peculiar, built-in conflict of a career in the self-help business: "It's a tricky business making money off of people's suffering," he said at one point, "but that's what I do."

My father had been worried that MCA would charge money

for the app, but he had convinced his boss, Jon, to give it away by telling him, "You can't buy that kind of goodwill." This had worked, but Jon occasionally became torn and would ask my father, "How do we make money off of this?" And my father would say, "We don't." Jon eventually internalized this oft-repeated conversation and began to have it with himself. I watched him ping-pong painfully between a human being's natural compassion and a businessman's self-interest. Almost in the same breath, Jon would say to a soldier, "We want to give back. The military does so much for us," then turn to my dad and say with a grin, "You can't buy this kind of publicity." My father, having developed a delightful attention in his middle age to the extended metaphor, whispered to me, "Jon likes to wear the coat of philanthropy. But sometimes the coat gets too hot, and he has to take it off."

At moments, an unbearable heaviness fell over our booth. A soldier came by and said a member of his unit had killed himself. Another soldier came up and said, "I need this app after the video I just saw." He described an educational video about sexual assault where a trainee was badly berated. "I wanted to kill myself after I saw that," he said, not entirely lightheartedly. I understood. I had watched the Army's antisuicide video, called "Shoulder to Shoulder: I Will Never Quit on Life." It was unbelievably depressing. It's heartbreaking to watch people talk about how they tried and failed to kill themselves. In the words of one soldier, "I took my gun. I put it to my chin. I put it on semi. And I pulled the trigger."

Even though my father had often told me he struggled emotionally during the development of the app, he seemed further moved by the stories of the soldiers. "People know someone," he said, "and that makes it real. When you work in isolation, it becomes theoretical."

My father especially liked that the app had the potential to reach a far larger group of people than any individual could. The exponential math is precisely what encourages him to create self-help products. I think there is another, unconscious attraction: not only can you help more people, you never have to meet those people. You never have to know about those who could not be helped.

"If you try to stop one person from committing suicide, it may work; it may not work," he told me. "But if you have an audience of ten thousand, you're going to save at least one person's life, maybe more. It's easier to save the world than it is to save just one person."

Pretty much anytime we talked about the app my father repeated some version of this statement. I couldn't help thinking that there had been, in fact, one person my father wasn't able to save. Maybe it was easier to save the world than to save just one person; or maybe it was just easier for him.

9

CONSIDER THE KITTEN POSTER

What Kind of Life Is Worth Living

When I started this book I wanted to understand how people come to care about self-help, and why. Self-help has been around for thousands of years, and it has been adored and reviled for just as long. Is it a useful, even essential, component of our society? Is it deleterious? Why has it been around so long? What does it provide?

The self-help book is a reflection of the enduring concerns and changing social needs of its time. During World War II, self-help titles included *Psychology for the Fighting Man, How the Jap Army Fights,* and *Handbook for Army Wives & Mothers.* A book helping readers identify silhouettes of airplanes—titled *What's That Plane*—sold about 400,000 copies. Even when self-help's offerings seem deluded and detrimental, like the New Thought movement's "mind cures," it helps to consider a broader context. The medical practices of that time included bloodletting, leeches, and electric shocks. Backaches, indigestion, and insanity in women were thought to be diseases of the reproductive organs, and were treated with various injections into the uterus or cauterization, using little anesthetic. Personality disorders in women were sometimes treated with removal of the ovaries. From this perspective, mind cure looks like progress.

Books like *The Rules* and *The Secret*, two of my least favorites on this journey, are likewise reflections of our culture. What I dislike about them may not be their authors or argument but the dissonance I feel when I try to reconcile the world I live in with the one they present.

As Americans, self-help reflects our core beliefs: self-reliance, social mobility, an endless ability to overcome obstacles, a fair and equal pursuit of success, and the inimitable proposition that every single human being wants and deserves a sack of cash. An ideology that reflects what you already believe is bound to make you feel validated. Self-help and America concur that just by existing you have the capability to get what you want, as long as you can help yourself. If you can't help yourself, you should probably move to France.

What Mark Victor Hansen's seminar, the Rules seminar, a flying class, a grief camp, a fire walk, and making a vision board all have in common is a willingness to meet the world through faith. William James wrote that "no fact in human nature is more characteristic than its willingness to live on a chance." What drives and validates self-help is a religious conviction that our abilities are in some way congruent with some larger force in the universe.

As with any enterprise that asks for blind faith, there is potential for abuse. Self-help is not an entity with a governing body, a regulating board, or checks and balances. It is founded in feeling. Anyone can write a book about anything. Someone will always be willing to profit from human weakness. The most detrimental type of self-help is a closed system that discourages interaction with other points of view.

Isolation is the flaw in self-reliance. The existence of self-help in part reflects a reality that we are not always aided by others, but it also creates a condition in which we are less inclined to request help. In this way the industry both reflects and reinforces a politically conservative viewpoint that values opportunity for the individual over responsibility to the community. If you fail, it's your fault, and not our problem. As Clement Stone wrote, "it is [Negative Mental Attitude] that is holding them down, not the external handicap which they give as the cause of their failure." Or see 2012 Republican presidential nominee Mitt Romney, deriding the alleged "forty-seven percent" of tax-avoiding Americans "who believe that they are victims, who believe the government has a responsibility to care for them, who believe that they are entitled to health care, to food, to housing, to you-name-it."

If everyone looks out for themselves, who will help those who can't? A culture of solipsism can quickly become a culture of narcissism. At what point does looking out for number-one stop being a wholesome American value and start making you an asshole?

New studies suggest that unrealistic optimism is a widespread human trait. Desirable information may be encoded in a different part of our brain than undesirable information. According to a recent *New York Times* article, "The brain neurons of extreme optimists do not effectively encode undesirable information."

All of us would probably like to be slimmer, smarter, richer, more popular, more successful. To what extent should you accept yourself for who you are, and to what extent should you attempt to better yourself? In asking this, we bump up against the self's limitations and possibilities. In each of us exists a tension between the motivating power of hope and the practicality of acceptance. What is each of us capable of? When is it right to ask for help? When should we accept failure? Answering these questions would be impossible without engaging our understanding of the self, and our understanding of the self's relationship to the larger world. Buried in there is an ontological question about what kind of life is worth living.

Suffering isolates us. A self-help book suggests the presence of a community without real human interaction. Belonging to an imagined collective is preferable to total psychic isolation. The ability to dream and the infrastructure that supports that dream are ways for different and marginalized people to feel like they belong.

The feeling of being helped is real and powerful. It is a motivating force that temporarily makes us feel more in control, less helpless, less despairing. It has a religious quality, inspiring the individual to keep working, keep striving, and keep hoping against all odds.

Really horrible things happen to people. Really horrible things happen to adults, to children, to old people. A really horrible thing happened to my father and me. We agree as a society that mothers are not supposed to kill themselves. But sometimes they do. How can we assimilate this knowledge, so discordant with what we took to be true? How can we contain this information so that it feels manageable, because we need things to feel manageable in order to keep living? We need a process. We need structure to feel safe. We need a reason to hang in there.

Can even the most bastardized, laughable incarnations of self-help carry some kernel of redeeming value? Consider the kitten poster that hangs in my hardware store. Over the words "Hang In There," a fluffy white kitten clings to a branch. I have seen this poster so many times I am inured to its cuteness. We are bored by these familiar images; we feel they can have no relevance and meaning in our lives. But, still, that phrase, "hang in there." It has some resonance. Everyone over the age of fifteen has had at least one experience of enduring unpleasantness, an experience that these words, or the sentiment behind them, might assuage. I myself have said those three words to someone as recently as a month ago, and when I said them I really meant it. I believed that the person I was speaking to was going through a difficult time, and I believed that difficult time would not last forever. Instead of voicing a longer, complicated pontification that for good reason doesn't comfortably reside in everyday human-to-human speech, I simply said, "Hang in there." Because "hang in there" is short-hand for the idea that troubles, the majority of them anyway, will pass with time.

Hang in there is what I wish my mother had been able to do. Being depressed is painful, and when you are depressed it is impossible to imagine a time when you will not be depressed. It is difficult to find a reason to live. But depressed people are wrong. Depression prevents them from seeing anything but full depression ahead. If a depressed person could just get through their depression, if they could just *hang in there* . . .

That, I like to believe, is the true function of the kitten poster. The kitten poster reminds us of our capacity for perseverance, against all evidence. My mother was on the waiting list for a very good mental hospital. If she had lived a few more days or weeks, could she have been helped? Would she be alive now? I have no idea. But if I could time travel, I would go back to 1979, and I would sit by my mother's bed, and I would make myself very tiny so I could crawl into her ear, and I would repeat, first whispering and then shouting: *Hang in there, hang in there, hang in there . . .*

In WHICH MY FATHER and I BREAK INTO a CEMETERY

On a hot Monday in July, my father and I drove to the cemetery in Oxon Hill, Maryland, where both of our mothers are buried. We had never visited my mother's grave before. Though we had begun to talk about her more, it still felt like a strange and unnatural thing for us to do together.

Negotiating grief can be awkward and fraught with misunderstanding for parents and children in particular. In my edition of C. S. Lewis's *A Grief Observed* there is a foreword by Lewis's stepson that I found especially trenchant. Lewis had written, "I cannot talk to the children about her [his wife, their mother]. The moment I try, there appears on their faces neither grief, nor love, nor fear, nor pity, but the most fatal of all non-conductors, embarrassment. They look as if I were committing an indecency." In the foreword his stepson responds:

I was fourteen when Mother died and the product of almost seven years of British Preparatory School indoctrination. The lesson I was most strongly taught throughout that time was that the most shameful thing that could happen to me would be to be reduced to tears in public. British boys don't cry. But I knew that if [Lewis] talked to me about Mother, I would weep uncontrollably and, worse still, so would he.

I found this misunderstanding poignant, probably because it reminded me of everything gone unsaid and potentially misinterpreted between my father and me. My silence about my mother had in part been an attempt to protect my father from his own sadness. The words "worse still, so would he" echoed in my head.

It was July 27, exactly thirty years since the day my mother had died in 1979. As we drove up to the gates, midafternoon, I could see they were chained. It hadn't occurred to either of us to call ahead; we had assumed the cemetery would be open. Since we had driven five hours to get there, this seemed like exceptionally poor planning. We coasted the perimeter of the grounds until I noticed an opening in the gate on the north side of the cemetery. Someone had kicked a section of the iron bars askew, and they lay at a forty-five-degree angle, leaving a triangular portal. I pointed this out to my father.

"You're suggesting we break into a cemetery?" he asked.

"It's not really breaking in if someone already did the breaking," I said. "Besides, we're here." It had taken thirty years, and I wasn't about to turn back now. Many times I had questioned why I was writing this book, and if its only purpose was to start a dialogue between my father and me that led us to this moment, it was enough. Leaving would have felt like failure on every possible level.

"Okay." He shrugged.

We parked at a McDonald's across the road. Plastered in the window was a giant poster of a berry smoothie; enticing icy drops clung to a plastic cup.

"Do you want a smoothie?" my father asked.

I frowned. I felt like he was stalling.

"They're pretty good," he said.

The synagogue my great-grandparents had belonged to was in Chevy Chase, Maryland, but as the number of dead grew too large for the adjacent plot, a separate, larger piece of land had been purchased forty miles away. At the time, I am told, it was a peaceful, bucolic location. Over fifty years later, the cemetery bordered a busy thoroughfare, on the other side of which numerous fast-food chains had sprung up. The neighborhood, if you could call it that, had a palpable, almost hostile inhabitability. It was a throughway, a place one passed through on the way to some other, hopefully nicer, place.

We walked along a concrete strip that served as a sidewalk in the oppressive July sun. Cars whizzed past, hazardously close. A corpulent woman and her infant waited for a bus; she regarded us with dagger eyes. My father, who habitually counters all adversity with a determined cheerfulness, greeted her warmly.

"Hello!" he said. "Beautiful baby."

She ignored us. My father shrugged.

For a moment, I wished that the dead had a better view than a McDonald's and a Dunkin' Donuts, but I then reminded myself they couldn't see. I was the one wishing for a nicer place to visit.

We ducked through the opening in the gate. My father couldn't remember exactly where our family was buried, so we wandered around. Occasionally, he would point to a family he had known. Finally, we stumbled onto the family plot.

"My mother used to come here on Father's Day, to visit her father," said my dad. "It irritated my father to no end." I felt for a moment the full weight of the concept; generations of my family visiting this spot. Would someone come visit me someday? It was an uncomfortable thought, though not the unhappiest of notions.

"It's nice that they're all here together," said my father, articulating a similar feeling. "My mother, her parents, my father, and Ellen."[*]

I looked at all the headstones. My great-grandfather and great-grandmother were here, as were my grandfather and grandmother, her brother, Danny, who had died of cancer at age thirty-six, and my mother. It struck me as anomalous that my mother was here among my father's family. My father could not remember how or why this had transpired.

"We were all in shock," was all he could offer as a reason.

My mother's gravestone was the smallest, a simple rectangle, flat against the ground. I calculated the difference between her birth and death date; she had been only thirty-one years old when she died. I was thirty-two. It was a bizarre concept, being older than my own mother, one that made me feel guilty and fortunate at the same time.

---

[*]Later that evening we would have dinner with my grandmother's salty, 84-year-old sister, who, after hearing my father express this same sentiment, would say pointedly, "There's no room for you. The last spot is mine."

"She was so young," I said to my father, and then I felt funny for having said it.

Engraved in the stone were the words

ELLEN R. SHAPIRO
1948–1979
BELOVED WIFE AND MOTHER

But what I actually read was

LEN R. SHAPIR
1948–1979
ELOVED WIFE AND

Grass had started to grow unevenly around the edges of the embedded stone, obscuring her name and the word "mother." Without speaking, my father and I crouched and began to remove the overgrowth. With bare hands, we brushed away dead leaves and blades of grass, pulled living grass and weeds from the ground. The physical contact felt good—the tension of the blades in my hands, the contraction of muscles in my arm, the force applied to separate roots from earth—and once I started weeding I felt like I couldn't stop. If someone had handed me a lawn mower at that moment I would have mowed a ten-foot radius around her gravestone. I might have mowed the entire cemetery. It was such a tangible symbol of neglect. No one had come to visit her in thirty years. Other graves had flowers by them, or small stones placed delicately on top.

In a campfire fable that had terrified me as a child, a man meets a beautiful woman with a yellow ribbon tied around her neck. He is quickly smitten. Several times, he asks about the ribbon. She won't explain why she wears it, but cautions him never to remove it. On their wedding night, after she falls asleep, he is overcome by curiosity. He carefully unties the ribbon. Her head falls off.

Remembering the story as an adult, and how immensely frightening it was to me, I realized what a terrible moral the story had. It was anti-curiosity, anti-knowledge; the punishment for wanting answers was beheading. The story had resonated with me, a child who wanted to know more about her mother but was afraid of upsetting her father. Curiosity killed, and one of my parents was already dead.

I had brought a small bouquet of wildflowers that I had tied together appropriately, I thought, with a yellow ribbon. I placed them on her newly cleaned grave, like I had seen so many people do in movies, but never in real life. My father and I stood up and stared at the stone. He started to cry. "It's so sad," he said. I didn't know what I was supposed to say. *Worse still, so would he.* It was one of those familiar moments where I could feel an old habit kick in. I could feel myself trying to flee, to avoid my feelings rather than acknowledge them. I felt stupid. I started to cry, and I wasn't sure if the tears were for my mother, or tears of embarrassment. I wasn't sure if it mattered why I was crying. I thought of the cliché "Pull yourself together." Usually, it is an admonition that means stop blubbering like an idiot, and this is initially why it came to mind. But I started to think of it as "Pull your selves together." As in: here is one self that wants badly to escape, and here is another self that is trying to stay, as I had read in so many self-help books, "in the moment."

Instead of watching and waiting to see which self would win (which, by the way, neither ever does; they just struggle until they collapse from fatigue), *pull your selves together.* I put my arm around my father's shoulders, and he put his arm around mine. We pulled together. We were standing the way people do when posing for a photograph, and we were crying. It felt odd to be half hugging, until I realized we were both trying not to close the space between us, because it would exclude my mother. We were standing in a way that we could embrace and still face her. It was almost a family hug, as close as we could get.

ACKNOWLEDGMENTS

My most heartfelt thanks to the following people and organizations that helped me with this book:

Henry Dunow, Sarah Knight, Molly Lindley, Denise Roy, Amanda Murray, Mark Binelli, Julia Holmes, Melissa Weinberg, Wendy Greenwald, David Greenwald, Lawrence Shapiro, Dinaw Mengestu, Marcela Valdes, Henry Jones, Jessica Harris, Madeleine Kuhns, The MacDowell Colony, Inn at the Oaks, Brant Lake, The New York Foundation for the Arts, Gabe Hudson, Leslie Falk, Alison Brown, Judy Budnitz, Heidi Julavits, Andrew Leland, Ben Marcus, Sara Levine, The Believer, *The Allen Room at the New York Public Library, The Omega Teen Camp, Comfort Zone Camp, Cory D. Kidd, The White Plains Hospital Anxiety & Phobia Treatment Center, Judy Shaw, Vanessa Ferreira, Professor David Willey, Julia Rothman, Jason Frank Rothenberg, Jaime Costas, and especially David and Lola.*

BIBLIOGRAPHY

Aurelius, Marcus. *Meditations.* Translated by Maxwell Staniforth. London: Penguin, 1964.

Banting, William. *Letter on Corpulence, Addressed to the Public.* London: Harrison, 1864.

Bourke, Joanna. *Fear: A Cultural History.* Emeryville, CA: Shoemaker and Hoard (Avalon Publishing Group), 2006.

Byrne, Rhonda. *The Secret.* New York: Atria Books, 2006.

Canfield, Jack, and Mark Victor Hansen, ed. *Chicken Soup for the Soul: 101 Stories to Open the Heart and Rekindle the Spirit.* Deerfield Beach, FL: Health Communications, 1993.

Carnegie, Dale. *How To Win Friends and Influence People.* New York: Simon & Schuster, 1936.

Carré, Jacques, ed. *The Crisis of Courtesy: Studies in the Conduct-Book in Britain, 1600–1900.* Leiden: E. J. Brill, 1994.

Cheyne, George. *The English Malady, or A Treatise of Nervous Diseases of all Kinds, as Spleen, Vapours, Lowness of Spirits, Hypochondriacal, and Hysterical Distempers, Etc. In Three Parts . . . With the Author's own Case at large.* London: G. Strahan, 1733.

Clark, Dan. "Make It Come True," in *Chicken Soup for the Soul,* edited by Jack Canfield and Mark Victor Hansen, 146–7. Deerfield Beach, FL: Health Communications, 1993.

Coué, Emile. *Self Mastery Through Conscious Autosuggestion.* New York: American Library Service, 1922.

Cullen, Jim. *The American Dream: A Short History of an Idea That Shaped a Nation.* Oxford: Oxford University Press, 2003.

Darwin, Charles. "Biographical Sketch of an Infant," in vol. 2 of *Mind: A Quarterly Review of Psychology and Philosophy.* 1877.

Darwin, Charles. *The Expression of the Emotions in Man and Animals.* Minneapolis: Filiquarian Publishing, 2007.

"Despite *The Rules,* I Lost My Husband to a Bad Set of Teeth." Independent.ie (Dublin). October 20, 2004.

Didion, Joan. *The Year of Magical Thinking.* New York: Vintage, 2007.

Dresser, Annetta Gertrude. *The Philosophy of P. P. Quimby. With Selections from His Manuscripts and a Sketch of His Life.* Boston: C. H. Ellis, 1895.

Edelman, Hope. *Motherless Daughters: The Legacy of Loss.* Cambridge, MA: Da Capo Press, 2006.

Emerson, Ralph Waldo. *The Essential Writings of Ralph Waldo Emerson.* New York: Modern Library, 2000.

Farewell, Nina. *Every Girl Is Entitled to a Husband.* New York: Macfadden-Bartell, 1964.

Fein, Ellen, and Sherrie Schneider. *The Rules: Time-tested Secrets for Capturing the Heart of Mr. Right.* New York: Warner Books, 1995.

Franklin, Benjamin. *Autobiography and Other Writings.* Oxford: Oxford University Press, 1993.

Freston, Kathy. *Quantum Wellness: A Practical and Spiritual Guide to Health and Happiness.* New York: Weinstein Books, 2008.

Gabor, Zsa Zsa. *How to Catch a Man, How to Keep a Man, How to Get Rid of a Man.* New York: Doubleday, 1970.

Grosvenor, Benjamin. *The Mourner: Or, The Afflicted Relieved.* London: George Keith, 1765.

Harvey, Greg, PhD. *Grieving For Dummies.* Hoboken: Wiley Publishing, 2007.

Hill, Napoleon. *Think and Grow Rich.* Meriden, CT: The Ralston Society, 1937.

Hughes, Lynne B. *You Are Not Alone: Teens Talk About Life After the Loss of a Parent.* New York: Scholastic, 2005.

James, William. *The Varieties of Religious Experience: A Study in Human Nature.* London: Routledge, 2002.

"January's Stock Temptation." *New York Times.* January 18, 2013.

Kübler-Ross, Elisabeth. *On Death and Dying.* New York: Scribner, 1997.

Leidner, Robin. *Fast Food, Fast Talk: Service Work and the Routinization of Everyday Life.* Berkeley: University of California Press, 1993.

Lewis, C. S. *A Grief Observed.* New York: HarperCollins, 1994.

Locke, John. *Some Thoughts Concerning Education.* Vol. XXXVII, Part 1. The Harvard Classics. New York: P. F. Collier & Son, 1909–14

McGee, Micki. *Self Help, Inc.: Makeover Culture in American Life.* New York: Oxford University Press, 2007.

Moore, Lorrie. *Self-Help.* New York: Vintage, 2007.

"No Laughing Matter." *Psychology Today.* July 1, 2006.

Patrick, Simon. *A Consolatory Discourse to Prevent Immoderate Grief for the Death of our Friends.* London: Francis Tyton, 1671.

Peale, Norman Vincent. *The Power of Positive Thinking.* New York: Fireside (Simon & Schuster), 2007.

Post, Emily. *Etiquette in Society, in Business, in Politics and at Home.* New York: Funk and Wagnalls, 1922.

Rush, Benjamin. "Of Grief," in *Medical Inquiries and Observations upon the Diseases of the Mind.* Philadelphia: Grigg and Elliot, 1835.

Schatzman, Morton. *Soul Murder: Persecution in the Family.* New York: Random House, 1973.

Skinner, B. F. "Baby in a Box." *Ladies' Home Journal,* October 1945.

Smiles, Samuel. *Self-Help: with Illustrations of Character and Conduct.* Boston: Ticknor and Fields, 1859.

Starker, Steven. *Oracle at the Supermarket: The American Preoccupation with Self-Help Books.* New Brunswick, NJ: Transaction Publishers, 2009.

Stone, W. Clement (with Napoleon Hill). *Success Through a Positive Mental Attitude.* New York: Prentice Hall, 1960.

"The Real Transformers." *New York Times.* July 29, 2009.

Tocqueville, Alexis de. *Democracy In America.* Translated by Harvey C. Mansfield and Delba Winthrop. Chicago: The University of Chicago Press, 2000.

Towne, Elizabeth. *Practical Methods for Self-Development: Spiritual, Mental, Physical.* Whitefish, MT: Kessinger Publishing, 2004.

Watson, John B. *Behaviorism.* New York: W. W. Norton, 1924.

Wattles, W. D. *The Science of Getting Rich.* Holyoke, MA: Elizabeth Towne, 1910.

Wood, Henry. *Ideal Suggestion Through Mental Photography: A Restorative System for Home and Private Use, Preceded by a Study of the Laws of Mental Healing.* Boston: Lee and Shepard Publishers, 1893.

ABOUT THE AUTHOR

Jessica Lamb-Shapiro writes fiction and nonfiction. A graduate of Brown University (BA) and Columbia University (MFA), she has published work in *The Believer, McSweeney's, Index Magazine,* and *Open City,* among others. She has received fellowships from The Mac-Dowell Colony and New York Foundation for the Arts (NYFA). She lives in New York City and Columbia County, New York.